A LIFELONG JOURNEY · THE ART AND TEACHING OF

H.G. GLYDE

PATRICIA AINSLIE

WITH AN INTRODUCTION BY HELEN COLLINSON

GLENBOW MUSEUM · CALGARY, ALBERTA, CANADA

A LIFELONG JOURNEY · THE ART AND TEACHING OF H.G. GLYDE

This volume has been produced by the
GLENBOW MUSEUM, CALGARY
with the assistance of the
CANADA COUNCIL, the
PROVINCE OF ALBERTA, and the
CITY OF CALGARY.

Glenbow Museum
130—9th Avenue S.E.,
Calgary, Alberta
Canada T2G 0P3

Cover:
Manoeuvres
(Currie Barracks Road), 1943
oil on canvas
cat. no. 25

H.G. GLYDE

CONTENTS

ACKNOWLEDGEMENTS

Henry Glyde is the key player in the development of art in Alberta over a thirty year period beginning in 1935. This is the first major exhibition of his art in many years, and the only one to document his entire career. By including student work and work made in England before he settled in Canada, it has been possible to show his roots and plot his progress from these early beginnings.

Glenbow has long been committed to producing an H.G. Glyde retrospective exhibition. An exhibition proposed in the early 1980s unfortunately had to be cancelled due to research and work already in progress outside of the museum. Glenbow has been very pleased to revive this long overdue project.

In preparing this exhibition I have had support and encouragement from many quarters. To all of those involved, I would like to extend my sincere thanks.

I have seen an enormous number of works by Henry Glyde in private hands. I would like to thank all those who so kindly gave me access to their collections and allowed me to photograph works. In some cases these collectors knew Glyde and related their knowledge of the artist to me. Without this access to private collections, affording a view of the range and depth of Glyde's work, such an exhibition would not be possible.

Public institutions made works by Glyde available to me and provided documentation and information. I wish to thank the Canadian War Museum, the National Gallery of Canada, Government House (Edmonton), Alberta Culture, the Edmonton Art Gallery, and all the staff of the University of Alberta Collections (Ring House Gallery). The latter has substantial holdings of Glyde's work. The Curator of Ring House, Helen Collinson, through Janine Andrews, Registrar, afforded me access both to the Glyde inventory at Ring House and Glyde's work dispersed around the university campus and in storage. I sincerely thank them both.

Helen Collinson, daughter of the artist, has contributed in diverse ways. She provided many insights on her father and the family's life in Canada, as well as a range of ideas on the sources for his style. She helped me to identify his associates and friends and provided me with exhibition information. As well, we spent many hours going through her own collection of Glyde's work. For all her support, interest, and enthusiasm I would like to extend my sincere appreciation and gratitude. She has also made a valuable contribution to the catalogue in the form of an introduction.

Henry Glyde gave generously of his time to provide in-depth information and background for his ideas and work, through discussions and taped interviews during my visits. Exploring anyone's past is a very personal affair and throughout he has accepted the probing with good grace and forthrightness. For his patience and contribution I am indebted to him. The exhibition is immeasurably enriched by this involvement. I thank both Henry and Hilda Glyde for their kindness and hospitality during my visits. The exhibition is strengthened by loans from Glyde's own collection, particularly of early English work which is nowhere else available.

Due to Glyde's prolific output, and the fact that the exhibition encompasses a life's work, the selection for the exhibition has been a rigorous task and a great deal of good work has had to be omitted. I am extremely grateful to all the lenders who have agreed to loan works for the exhibition and long tour.

I would like to extend my gratitude to Glyde's associates and friends who talked at length to me, providing their insight into the art and life of Glyde. They agreed to taped interviews which make a key contribution to this exhibition, but also to future research on the artist and his time. Particularly, I thank Stanford Perrott, Stanford Blodgett, Grace Turner, Murray MacDonald, Marcel Asquin, Alison Forbes, Robert Willis, Paul Gishler, Francis Winspear, Colleen Millard, Norman Yates, Harry Kiyooka, and Elsie Park Gowan.

There are many others who have given assistance. Particularly I would like to thank James Parker and Gertrude McLaren at the University of Alberta Archives, who helped me locate an extremely useful and important body of material in various papers in the archives. Jetske Ironside, Professor of Art History, University of Alberta, with her broad knowledge of Alberta art history, provided important background information, particularly on the Alberta Society of Artists. Thanks are due to Dr. Naomi Jackson Groves for providing material from the Jackson papers, and Frances Smith for locating relevant material on André Biéler. Dr. Robert Lamb was also helpful. Libraries across Canada have provided information from biographical files. The Royal College of Art, the Brassey Institute, the Bank of England, the Victoria and Alberta Museum Library, and the National Gallery of Canada Library and Archives have been helpful.

I extend special thanks to Rod Green at Masters Gallery in Calgary. He has been of enormous assistance in helping me track down paintings and has arranged for me to see work in private collections. I would also like to acknowledge my appreciation to Masters Gallery for its exposure and continued support for important early Alberta artists, such as Marion Nicoll and Henry Glyde.

I extend special thanks to Victoria Baster who had done the earlier, initial exploration for the Glyde exhibition at Glenbow. Her careful reading and valuable suggestions and ideas has contributed significantly to the manuscript. It has been a pleasure once more to work with Rose Veighey whose thorough and sensitive editing has successfully combined the two manuscripts. The designer of the catalogue, Mary Jameson, has organized the material with insight and forethought.

The physical mounting of this exhibition has involved a carefully synchronized collective effort to which many members of the museum's professional staff have made important contributions. To all of them I extend my sincere thanks. The photography for the exhibition, by Jim Shipley was co-ordinated by Katherine Lipsett who also assisted with other details. Valerie Robertson and Christopher Jackson proofread the catalogue. Lindsay Moir assisted with the bibliography. Ewa Smithwick and Ann Gardner did important and, in some cases, delicate conservation work. Works on paper were matted by Gordon Duggan and Tawny Kohut and all new framing was completed by Terry Hagan. Shipping and the tour was co-ordinated by Daryl Betenia, Larry Hoffner, and Linda Kurtz. Kay Bridges and Lise Dufresne typed the manuscript which was typeset by Luana Russell. Harry Beaver co-ordinated the installation of the exhibition by Brian King, Rod Bennett, Ivan Zadravic, and Dan Doyle in the galleries.

I would like to thank Duncan F. Cameron, Director, and the Board of Governors for their support for the project. The Canada Council, the Government of Alberta, and the City of Calgary have made a generous contribution to this exhibition and catalogue. May I add my personal thanks for their ongoing support.

Patricia Ainslie
Curator of Art
Glenbow Museum

Vegreville Skyline, 1937
watercolour on paper
cat. no. 12

A SENSE OF PLACE • BY HELEN COLLINSON

"Without a past that is malleable as well as generously preserved, the present will lack models to inspire it and the future be deprived of a lifeline to its past."[1]

Over half a century has passed since my parents arrived, in 1935, for a year's stay in the romantic Canadian west. They had come on the train from Montreal with their assorted belongings, which included me, a nine-month-old baby with the measles. On the September day we reached Calgary, it was hot, windy, and searingly bright. The dusty, dry, autumn afternoon only confirmed the discomfiture and unease they had felt as they crossed this huge land, through the forests of northern Ontario and then over the broad plains. Canada seemed incomprehensibly large, wild, and empty, devoid of the human habitation which, for them, meant civilization itself. That day my mother reacted negatively to the heat and the dust, and remembers still the unfamiliar, dry, gritty taste which contributed to an oppressive sense of rawness that permeated the centre of the town. Because I was quite ill and liable for quarantine, we were cloistered in the Balmoral Hotel, where I was generously and tenderly cared for by a medical doctor who remained our dear friend throughout his life.[2]

This short anecdote illustrates the polarities that seem to epitomize my parents' relationship with Canada. To this day, they feel a strong tie to the land and the culture of the England that they left fifty years ago. They still respond to its cultivated, tamed countryside which is quaintly dotted with small towns and divided by hedgerows. It is a country full of the activity of both the past and the present, and crowded with people for whom history is part of everyday life.

In my parents' eyes, Calgary in 1935 seemed a tough place. Its residents proudly exhibited the rough edges which were clearly visible in many small ways. In this frontier town in a new country, people were genuinely caring about their friends, their neighbours, and newcomers. My parents arrived without the slightest understanding of the bold friendliness, the lack of reticence, the openness, the guilessness, and the curiosity that they encountered. They both have spoken often about this friendliness, the generosity, the warmth, and honest concern that was accorded them. The other side of the coin was their confusion and withdrawal in the face of overwhelming interest and enthusiasm. For my father, these attitudes became problematic upon occasion. He simply did not understand what was so interesting and endlessly fascinating about being an artist, nor did he comprehend the "romantic artist" as an eccentric character with some kind of mysterious status. He often desired the anonymity that he believed still possible in England.

Like many new Canadians, however, my father quickly responded to the challenge of becoming a part of the cultural life of this country, and he contributed all he could in his chosen field. His sense of place and his personal milieu were central to his work, and developed as he defined his relationship with Canada and specifically Alberta.

Soon after our arrival in Calgary, there was a trip into the countryside towards Cochrane to visit A.C. Leighton and his wife, Barbara, at their home. My father had come to Calgary at the invitation of Leighton, who had been a friend and sketching companion in Hastings when my father was a young student. The roads terrified my father. He laughs now at his innocence and naiveté because the reason for his concern was the noise of the gravel (as large as small boulders, he claims) battering the bottom of the flimsy car as it clattered through the dark at breakneck speed. Since then, of course, we have our own stock of stories about how it took ten hours to get from Banff to Radium in wet weather and the marvellous engineering of the switchbacks on the ''Big Hill'' north of Saskatchewan Crossing.

I remember Leighton's particular hat and western clothes. His wife always wore jodhpurs. I remember feeling shocked to see her thus attired at the funeral of one of her, and our, dearest friends. Now, it seems simply honest behaviour. Leighton himself was a colourful personality who was adored and idolized by many of his pupils and, as the nephew of Lord Leighton, played up the mystique of the famous artist from England. The romance that Leighton felt about this country was related, I have always thought, to gentlemanly adventure. He was the intrepid explorer. Hence, like so many other people who loved the land, he travelled and camped in the mountains. Also he seemed like a brave, flamboyant artist, and traveller who painted to interpret the vast romantic landscape for those at home. My father is a romantic too, and Canada trapped him and caught his heart entirely, but he felt a wholly different pull. He was not an intrepid adventurer. Rather, he felt the challenge of the developing culture and saw vast potential in this new country. He responded to the people — the early pioneers, the country doctors, and the farm women. He was humbly respectful and awed by their accomplishments.

He did not relish the idea of sleeping on the ground in a tent nor did he care to climb great heights roped together with fellow climbers. He thought that riding horses for pleasure bordered on insanity and I know of only one occasion when he was on a horse.

''In the summer of 1936 R.L. Harvey invited me to go up to Bow Lake. The road had been cut just beyond Bow Lake and Peyto Lake was accessible only by horse. We went along a precipice on these horses and I remember saying, 'How do you stop this bally thing?' and the guide said, 'Never mind, he knows what he's doing even if you don't. Just sit there.' ''[3]

In England, my father used to go out sketching with A.C. Leighton and together they painted many of the picturesque windmills that were so common in the Sussex countryside. These watercolours were executed within the English landscape tradition derived from Cox, De Wint, and Cotman. Leighton's ultimate interest lay in his command of the formal qualities of watercolour painting.

Indeed, Leighton's subsequent work is readily understood in the romantic context of the English Picturesque tradition,[4] and his Canadian landscapes reveal this adherence to these English roots. His obvious delight in the wildness of the land and the vastness of the clear Canadian sky is translated onto paper with consummate skill. Although he combined keen observation with his essentially romantic stance, Canada was interpreted through English eyes and his aesthetic point of view remained wedded to that which had inspired his English watercolours prior to his move to Canada in 1929.

Although my father shared an interest in watercolour painting with Leighton in England, the concept of the picturesque did not remain central to his development as an artist. Long before he came to Calgary, his inclinations were more directed to an English tradition quite different from that which motivated Leighton.[5] My father had always been capable of imaginative fantasy. Thus, his work often contained a literary connection and sometimes his drawings were passionately convoluted in a manner similar to the work of Fuselli, Blake, or the Pre-Raphaelites. Although the Pre-Raphaelites often used exotic subject matter, they also attempted to paint realistically and paid great attention to detail.

Speaking of his relationship with this aspect of English painting, my father has indicated that: ''Ordinary things really appeal to me. Much of my work may appear flamboyant but that is the flamboyance of the small things around you.''[6] By the time he left England, his interests in figure painting, mural decoration, and allegorical subject matter were all firmly part of his point of view. He was a consummate draughtsman and he brought this sensibility with him to Canada.

There are many sources for these ideas and attitudes. At the Brassey Institute, which he attended full-time from 1923 to 1926, he was exposed to a combined fine and decorative art curriculum. There he met Christopher Nevinson, who by this time had renounced his association with the Vorticists. Even so, he did introduce my father to the work of the Italian Futurists and, through the filter of British interpretation, awakened his consciousness to some contemporary European trends.

My father, however, felt that he had been isolated in Hastings and has often likened this isolation to that which he felt in Canada. Obviously, the distances are not comparable, but he has said he felt the connections to what was going on in other parts of the world continued to be very important to him while he was in Canada. Because of World War Two and a variety of other outside reasons, it was 1949 before he had an opportunity to return to England for a three-month visit.

My father attributes his continuing interest in the work of William Roberts and Stanley Spencer to his early contact with Nevinson. He sees this influence particularly in the sense of composition, the ''stacking'' of forms, and the forward tilt of the pictorial space which is so characteristic of Spencer. However, this compositional attribute may also be linked to an avid interest in the early Renaissance that was kindled when my father went to the Royal College of Art in 1926.

It was here that he became acquainted with the technique, the aesthetic and the iconography of Cimabue. He was also deeply affected by the use of the human figure, both iconographically and as a formal element, in the work of Piero Della Francesca. The latter's composition introduced a solid, three-dimensional quality compared to the more static, planar characteristics of the earlier Italian, Cimabue.

All these different influences and interests have characteristics in common. Roberts, Spencer, the early Italians, and even the Futurist works are all strongly linear. The colour used tends to be local and specific. Further, any abstract qualities that are present are fairly obviously derived from representations of objects.

My father's arrival in Canada did not significantly alter these elements, which were part of his personal artistic beliefs, and a case can be made for the proposition that he simply tackled painting in this new country with the tools that he brought with him from England. This would, of course, be a logical assumption to make. Although it is to be expected that changes take place over time in new surroundings, certain basics have remained relatively constant.

My father's work has been compared to some American art of the late 1920s and the 1930s.[7] At that time, there was a strong movement (particularly in the mid-west) towards the creation and definition of a specifically American cultural identity. The art that was produced was variously known as ''New American'' painting, ''regionalist art'' or ''regionalism,'' and it owed much to local, environmental factors. Artists as diverse as Thomas Hart Benton, Charles Burchfield, and Grant

Hilda and Henry Glyde,
Canmore, 1940s

Wood were associated with this movement, most particularly by writers and critics. The movement was variously associated with both left and right wing political elements.

Ultimately, a true "regionalist" school did not develop and the American efforts were later regarded negatively. However, the idea of art which is truly indigenous and informed by definable physical and cultural environments is with us still, and the term "regionalism" is used to discuss it. We seem to have developed a wider and more general context than in the thirties, however.[8]

The association of my father's work with this "New American" painting is easy to understand if one compares his stylistic characteristics with those of Benton, for example. There is present in both a strong narrative content, the use of local colour, and the expressionistic presence of swirling figures with a definite linear emphasis.

However, Benton's work has a rough-hewn quality and a clipped, frenetic line that seems to come from a rhythm closely related to jazz. The quality of light in his work is demonstrably dramatic. By contrast, my father's surfaces tend to be fine and detailed. His line is flowing, sinuous, and reminiscent of elongated melodic tunes more in the Baroque tradition than associated with syncopated modernism. He does not often make use of overtly dramatic light. Most importantly, he does not illustrate the specific folklore of the countryside. Even though he may set his work in a particular locality, he is apt to be interested in a general statement. The landscape itself is not one of his symbols.

My father was very interested in the concept of regionalism, however, and he used to speak about it often. He used the term "regional" while encouraging his pupils to express themselves as directly as they could, and to take for inspiration those things of life around them that they knew the best. He felt that such activity would result in a particularly Canadian, perhaps western Canadian, expression and that in helping to build this framework he would be contributing something of great importance and interest. He was convinced of the necessity for a grass-roots base and felt that artists would not be able to stay in Alberta and work at their art until there was community support.

"...It was around 1880 that a British R.A. pointed out that the salvation of Canadian Art was to have something Canadian, or shall we say, something grown up from the soil — not the imitation of something completely foreign. This holds today. We shall not get anywhere if we lean too heavily upon designs we do not understand.

"... Modern work is being done at the moment in the studio, and once we start following something that has already been done, we can't hope to be the originator or the top man. Tru-

ly, our study of painting that has gone before is most essential, but if it is to be studied properly, one discovers that it is a product of its own time and of its country or community, and you cannot possibly mistake a Frenchman for an Italian, or a Brueghel for a Grunewald."[9]

In this sense, he had a real mission as a teacher in western Canada and he encouraged his pupils to be aware of their surroundings and to express their own particular realities. It was in this spirit that he participated so enthusiastically in the early rural art classes sponsored by the Department of Extension of the University of Alberta.

He has now lived in western Canada for most of his life and he would say that it is completely natural that he makes use of some local elements in his work. In this sense my father could be called a regionalist. He has not, however, used the Canadian landscape as a symbol in itself and he remains somewhat as a disinterested observer. He described his feelings about this point as follows:

"I don't really feel I am a landscape painter although the ruggedness of the landscape here appealed to me very much. These huge rocks... [the mountains]... were a real challenge and much of my stuff was constructed... [rather than being "drawn" or "placed"]... on paper.

"I think that the 'Canadian' stuff in that narrow sense is extremely limited. A.Y. ...[Jackson]... and I approached things differently. There are 'Canadian Rhythms' typical of this land.

"I feel that my subject matter came to me before I met Jackson. I had a very deep friendship with him. He said to me once, 'Forget your drawing, forget your symbolism, concentrate on your landscapes.'

"Somehow he made a symbol of his landscape in a way that I never did. It was never a symbol for me in the same sense it was for him."

My father's early watercolours in Canada reflect a desire to record, fairly, accurately, and realistically, the character of the wild, beautiful, and sometimes monumental land around him. He was fascinated by the architecture of the soaring prairie grain elevators and, in calling them the "Cathedrals of the Prairie,"[10] likened them to the spires of churches in England. I remember him describing how the elevator signalled, miles in advance, the presence of a town here in Alberta in much the same way as the cathedral spire did in England. He admired the simple, functional architecture that stood proudly on the flat plains, giving definition and character to so many small western Canadian hamlets.

It is worthwhile to note perhaps, that his reaction to the grain elevator was somewhat ambiguous. He did not articulate the absolute meaning of such a structure as did A.M. Klein when he concluded "It's because it's bread. It's because bread is its theme, an absolute."[11] However, my father did accord this particular structure a great deal of importance, and its presence in paintings such as *The Exodus* and *Aftermath* seems to denote more than a simple identification of place.

The ambiguity of observing while not participating is evident in *Skaters* which he painted soon after his arrival. It is a somewhat bucolic and descriptive canvas and, in a very real sense, the work of a disinterested observer. He never did become accustomed to the severe winters and was not a sportsman. He has never learned to skate although he admires the skill of hockey and the speed of the players. He has drawn hockey games and tried to capture the grace and agility of the game.

In a similar way, from a real distance, he saw and recorded the fine carriage, the high cheekbones, and fine chiselled features of the Stoney Indians. He responded to their sense of dignity and pride as he felt it was exemplified in any dealings that he had with them at Banff. He had a profound empathy with their social conditions but they remained, however, people from whom he felt far removed. He represented them in his mural *Alberta History* in a classical style and with proud bearing. In the low relief that he did for the City Hall in Edmonton, the Indian people were represented by immense profiles, static, stoic, and god-like in their demeanour.

Initially, although he did not personally feel a full member of Canadian society, my father felt that there was much for Canadians to be proud of and he was avidly interested in the art that had been produced in this country. He found it difficult to accept western Canadians' diffidence about their own artistic creativity.

There were, indeed, many things for my father to adjust to. For instance, he was hired to teach people how to draw and to do this he needed a live, nude model. One day Dr. Carpenter, the Head of the Provincial Institute of Technology and Art, came to see him to discuss the problem that having nude models was causing in the community. While Dr. Carpenter was very sympathetic about the need for models, he had a difficult public relations problem to handle. Finally he asked my father if the girl had to be completely nude. "Could she not wear an ankle bracelet? Surely this would not interfere with the artistic activity." When my father asked how this could possibly solve the problem, Carpenter replied that, when the ladies asked if

South of Lethbridge, 1940
watercolour
on paper
cat. no. 18

the models had anything on, he could truthfully answer "yes" and he was sure this would satisfy them.

Such issues were not merely amusing to my father. These ideas stemmed from attitudes that became a source of anger and upset. He felt that many times his teaching was genuinely interfered with and that his paintings were sometimes judged on moralistic grounds. There grew in him a real feeling of dichotomy and an ambivalence about Alberta. Such feelings did not entirely disappear even when we moved to Edmonton in 1946 to a welcome association with the University of Alberta.

My parents were ambitious and had a strong belief in the importance of intellectual capabilities as well as an eagerness for the multiplicity of ideas that the world of books and learning offered. In addition, my father has an admiration for intelligence, knowledge and learning, effort, and hard work. These characteristics have been constant factors and his work habits attest to this.

He loves drawing and still draws every day, as I remember him doing since I was a child. No matter how small a house we lived in, he always had a studio. He was there often after supper and nearly all day Saturday and Sunday. Our vacations, too, (crowded in between the end of the summer session at Banff and the beginning of the children's school) were painting trips. We often spent these two weeks in Canmore which was one of my father's favourite haunts. Each day, we packed a picnic lunch and either walked or drove to a likely sketching spot. Our days were filled with simple activities such as wading in mountain streams, climbing scree slopes, looking for strawberries, or reading while my father did his oil sketches and filled notebooks with pencil sketches. Those were often idyllic times. It was rarely that we met other people in the out-of-the-way spots we visited. It was like having a series of perfect gardens all to ourselves.

Although, throughout his life, art has been my father's prime motivation, he still reads a great deal and loves music. He sang in a choir in Calgary and also in Edmonton and he took great pride in his tenor voice. He had received a classical musical training as a choirboy in England and this has remained with him.

He has also been very interested and involved in the theatre both as an actor and designer. Musical theatre was not a common occurrence although he did have two notable successes. One of my earliest memories of my father playing the fool was in a production of "Naughty Marietta" before we left Calgary. He had the male lead, I think, and at one point he flubbed his lines. The cover-up was magnificient and only the "chosen few" knew of his disgrace. That evening was a revelation to me, however,

for my father had been transformed on the stage into a total stranger.

Beginning in 1936, six weeks of each summer were spent in Banff. Throughout the war years and for several years afterwards, we rented a large, rambling cabin at the end of Cave Avenue very close to the Cave and Basin swimming pools. It had four bedrooms and at least eight large beds. The kitchen was dominated by a huge coal and wood stove which my long-suffering mother cursed roundly. My most pervasive memory is of wonderful talk, arguments and laughter, and a steady stream of interesting visitors. I don't know what the pupils at the Banff School took home with them after six weeks in the mountains. Certainly, many of the Faculty members participated fully. In retrospect, it was a very special time.

In 1949, my father and mother returned to England for a three-month visit. Upon his return to Edmonton, my father painted a number of important canvases. One of these paintings *Prairie Couple* has a unified quality that is perhaps the best expression of his feeling about his adopted home. *Prairie Couple* combines figure and landscape and, although the former is definitely dominant, there is a pervasive sense of the feeling of western Canada as a backdrop. There is a church in the background, the only identifiable architectural form.[12] It is a simple composition that expresses a sense of stability, with both vertical and horizontal elements present. Feelings of struggle or disharmony are thus minimized.

A man and woman stand behind a thick rustic, rough-hewn fence. The male figure stands behind his wife and could be interpreted as either supportive or merely an echo of the dominant form of the woman. The presence of the sturdy fence seems to underline the fortitude and loyalty of the couple one to the other. The fence also creates a massive barrier between the couple and the viewer. It is a structure of their own making, however, and could also be interpreted as a protection from the harshness of the land in which they have chosen to live.

Although *Prairie Couple* is a small painting, it seems to contain a resolution of many of my father's visual and philosophical concerns. It may well be a self portrait. Certainly it is a tribute to the fastness and importance of a central relationship, and it celebrates the basic human traits of faith, hope, and love. It seems to represent a successful expression of the oneness that my father has come to feel with this country and, in some real sense, stands as his tribute to its people.

NOTES

1. David Lowenthal. *The Past is a Foreign Country*. (Cambridge: Cambridge University Press, 1985), 411.
2. Dr. Earle Scarlett later became the Chancellor of the University of Alberta and I was privileged to receive my B.A. Degree from him personally.
3. Collinson interview with Glyde in 1972. I do not remember ever seeing my father on a horse. On the trip described above, however, he did a little pencil drawing of the horse which belonged to the guide, Bill Neish. This drawing is now in the collections of the Whyte Museum of the Canadian Rockies.
4. For a general discussion of the picturesque and the sublime as it applies to British watercolour painting see: *Turner and the Sublime*, by Andrew Wilton. (London: British Museum, 1980), 31.
5. Nikolaus Pevsner, *The Englishness of English Art* (Harmondsworth: Penquin, 1964).
6. Glyde to Collinson.
7. John Bentley Mays, "Art history of Alberta tells story of isolation," *Globe and Mail*, 6 August 1980.
8. A series of exhibitions at The Harbourfront Art Gallery in Toronto have explored regionalism recently. In his introduction to the latest catalogue, William Boyle states: "Many of our curators, fully conversant in the international idiom, have chosen to explore their own backyard and to build from the strength of what they know best. This has produced a confident and expansive regionalism at polar opposites from the pejorative sense of the word."
Boyle later quotes Northrop Frye, "Within the last twenty years we have been seeing more and more areas of this huge and sparsely settled country become culturally visible through painters and writers who belong, as creative people, less to Canada than to the prairies, Pacific coast, the Atlantic coast, southern Ontario or Quebec..." [Northrop Frye, *Divisions on a Ground*, (Toronto: House of Anansi Press, 1982), 17]. Quoted in the introduction to Joan Borsa, *Another Prairies*, Exhibition Catalogue, (Toronto: The Art Gallery at Harbourfront, 1986).
9. Henry George Glyde. From an unpublished radio talk manuscript from the series "University of the Air" c.1957.
10. This expression has been attributed to A.Y. Jackson. I don't know who used the expression first.
11. A.M. Klein, "The Grain Elevator." *Canadian Poetry in English*, (Toronto: Ryerson Press, 1954), 372.
12. A grain elevator would have served to place the location of the painting in western Canada but this was obviously not his prime motive. The presence of the church is important in any analysis of the meaning of the work, which remains personal.

Prairie Couple, 1950
egg tempera and oil on
wood panel
cat. no. 52

Self Portrait, 1932
conté on paper
cat. no. 7

"Glyde was considered a gentle fellow and aristocratic. He was reserved but he had a jolly smile and friendly laugh and he was full of fun, very energetic, physically and mentally too. I was fascinated by his black and white stuff with minute, careful working over; his work was so precise, almost cold. He was inspiring and supportive. Glyde spent time convincing you that what you did had value. He left me with the impression that it [art] was a wonderful life."

Perrott

A LIFELONG JOURNEY • THE ART AND TEACHING OF H.G. GLYDE

"With its back lying hard against the eastern wall of the Rockies, we find a land which marks the end of the great plains, and introduces the rolling forms of the foothills, which buttress the huge precipitous ramparts that rise to the skies to terminate in the huge ice fields which lie beyond the clouds.

"Such is Alberta, over which are scattered many hamlets and small towns, but few cities.

"In the central portions, where the bushlands have been opened, there is a certain quiet beauty, and a certain snugness. Here are farm houses and log huts, nestling in the concavities of the contours, and, drawn over the hills, tightly knitted patterns of trees richly texturing the whole landscape.

"In contrast, there is the stark beauty of the southeast, with the dry yellow grasses stretching out to a hard horizon under the almost eternal white light of the sun. Practically all that lives struggles for existence: man is forever fighting the elements. Dead trees surround the paintless houses, with their weather boards ashened, buckled, and gaping. Against the sides rests the drifting sandy soil, thrown there by the hurricane winds of the chinook.

"Looking down on the vast medley of changing scenes are the huge, solid ranges of the Rockies, which fringe the western skyline, zigzagging their way into Canada's hinterland." [1]

Glyde, 1947

This was Glyde's vision of Alberta, where he lived for over thirty years and to which he made an important and lasting contribution.

A Main Camp,
Alaska Highway,
1944
watercolour over
pencil on paper
cat. no. 37

Glyde's art was rooted in concepts developed as a student in England in the 1920s. These links with modern British art were to remain an important element in his work. Philosophically, however, he was committed to the development of a truly Canadian art, based on direct observation and interaction with the landscape and people. His early figure painting in Canada, in a era that was essentially committed to landscape, was innovative. He laid emphasis on the figure as a means of exploring the Canadian spirit, and created a body of work that with its mythological and symbolic character broke new ground in the West.

During the period 1935 to 1966, Glyde was the single most important individual in the development of art teaching in Alberta. He developed fledgling programs in art at the Provincial Institute of Technology and Art in Calgary (now the Alberta College of Art) and the Banff School of Fine Arts. In 1946, he began the art program at the University of Alberta in Edmonton.

Besides these endeavours, he was also deeply involved in bringing art to the widespread communities of the province. From the late 1930s he taught art in the extension program of the University of Alberta in towns such as Vegreville, Lethbridge, and Medicine Hat.

In all his teaching, Glyde was determined not only to provide his students with a thorough grounding in the techniques of art but to enable them to see and think for themselves. Through his enthusiasm and energy, he not only established a place for art in Alberta, he created a realization of its relevance to contemporary life.

End of the Prairie, 1957
mixed technique on masonite
cat. no. 67

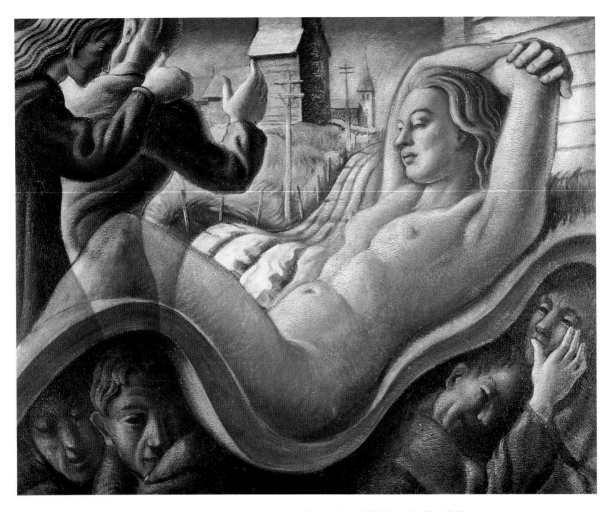

She Sat Upon a Hill Above the City, 1949
mixed technique on cardboard
cat. no. 49

Seated Figure, 1959
oil on panel
cat. no. 72

Highway No. 2 Going North, 1960
oil on canvas
cat. no. 75

ENGLAND • THE EARLY YEARS

Henry George Glyde was born on 18 June, 1906 in Luton, Bedfordshire, England. When he was three years old the family moved to Hastings, on the south coast of England. Glyde's father was originally from Hastings and Geo and his three younger brothers grew up surrounded by five generations of Glydes. Though Hastings was an extremely old town, it had remained small and linked to the rural and primarily agricultural life of Sussex. At a very early age, Glyde developed a deep and abiding love for the land.

The area was also rich in architecture and Glyde benefited greatly from the opportunity to see and experience it first hand. He especially loved the Norman Romanesque style churches of Sussex, "so warm and so closely knit to the earth with heavy rhythms. I felt that the architecture was near the life of everything."[2]

Glyde attended the local Church of England school. In 1920, at the age of fourteen, he wrote the examinations and won a scholarship to attend the Brassey Institute of Arts and Sciences. This was a part-time scholarship and in his first years at the Brassey, Glyde also worked with his father as a painter and decorator. In 1923, however, he enrolled as a full-time student.

Glyde's wish to study art was completely out of keeping with his family's tradition and expectations. In their eyes he was throwing away a practical trade for a chancy and unpromising career. However, his determination to attend the Brassey was based on a long held interest in

drawing and in form. "I was constantly drawing... Anything that was spare at all I used to draw on."[3] Glyde's earliest childhood memory was of modelling and working clay.

The Brassey Institute was a small school with a large part-time enrollment, but only about a dozen students in full-time classes. Built by Lord Brassey in 1879, the School of Art occupied the two top floors of the Institute over the library. The school reflected the conservative and provincial climate of Hastings. Glyde followed a thoroughly academic course. There was life drawing and a great deal of drawing from the antique. With his interest in architecture, Glyde did a lot of drawing from plaster casts of architectural fragments as well as casts of the figure. He also studied design. In the spring, the school took advantage of the beautiful natural surroundings with students doing much landscape work out-of-doors. Art History was introduced both in practical classes and as a separate course.

His main teachers were Philip Cole, Harry Tickner, and Leslie Badham who taught anatomy and landscape. The emphasis in the teaching at the Brassey was on drawing in line and tone. Colour was a secondary concern; painting was merely the colouring of a drawing. Tone and not colour was used to denote contour and space.

The instruction at the Brassey Institute followed along the lines of the Royal College of Art in London with which it was connected. Students at the Brassey, as at art schools in other provincial towns, could write entrance examinations and enter the Royal College. Glyde did this in 1926 and won a scholarship to attend.

The Royal College undertook to provide a thorough technical training for advanced students of art, and to provide professional training for art teachers as a post-diploma course. Upon completion of the courses, a Diploma of Associateship was awarded, which allowed the graduate to use the letters A.R.C.A. after his name.

There were five schools in the college. Glyde entered the School of Design but also took courses in the School of Drawing and Painting. He completed the three-year Diploma course and an additional post-diploma year in mural and decorative painting.

In his first year at the college, Glyde took life drawing, architecture, and design. He studied the human figure and still life with an emphasis on composition and form, and was regularly required to complete figure compositions. His preferred painting medium at this time was gouache. Lectures on technique and history of art and architecture were held at the Victoria and Albert Museum and at the Slade. With other students, Glyde would attend these and also special lectures. For example, Eric Gill lectured on engraving. Glyde visited the galleries, including the Tate, to see new work. The rich and diverse collections at the Victoria and Albert Museum were particularly inspiring.

By his second year, Glyde had begun to specialize in mural design with courses in technique and chemistry with E. Dinkel. He continued life drawing with Walter Monnington, a young artist, and Randolph Schwabe who, in addition to life drawing, taught imaginative and memory drawing. This was important training for work in illustration. Glyde was very impressed by the skill and expressiveness of one of the older drawing instructors, Constable Alston. William Rothenstein, who was principal of the college, gave occasional criticisms and his work was seen by the students. Throughout all Glyde's courses there was a emphasis on technique, drawing, and design.

In his fourth year Mural and Decorative Painting course, Glyde was required "to practise the elements of Figure and Ornamental Design, and to study the methods and processes necessary for the thorough mastery of Painting and Decoration alike of a public and of a domestic character."[4] Emphasis was placed on mastery of various mural techniques using gesso grounds, egg tempera, casein, laying plaster, panel painting in oil, finishing, and gilding.

One of Glyde's most important teachers at the college was Ernest Tristram, who was an expert on English medieval murals and had done many restorations around the country. Glyde had already developed a strong personal interest in the art of the Romanesque and Gothic periods. He had grown up with an awareness of the English versions of these styles. Architectural fragments he had found had intrigued him. Tristram's direct link with church architecture and murals reinforced this interest of Glyde's.

With Tristram, Glyde studied the design and composition of murals, the brushwork used in various periods, and the fundamentals of such effects as the luminosity of colour. Tristram was a classicist who favoured a linear kind of design with figures outlined, not shown as volumes, with flat colour applied to fill the forms and some limited, delicate modelling. Principally a restorer, he did very little original work. Students could observe him working on cartoons for the murals in his studio at the college.[5]

Besides benefiting from instructors like Tristram, Glyde pursued his interest in medieval art independently, studying the French and Italian Romanesque and Gothic styles in London's libraries and museums. He developed a special interest in 13th and 14th century Italian Gothic art. The style varied from the linear-patterned, Byzantine-inspired style of Duccio (1268-1319) and Simone Martini (1284-1344) of Siena, to the more naturalistic, illusionistic work of Florence particularly evident in the work of Giotto (1266-1337).

He also liked the earlier, heavier style of southern France of the 12th century, in which it seemed to him that "art met the earth." These interests directed Glyde's early work at the college and had a continuing influence throughout his life. He felt that, using the approach from the art of this period, "I got nearer to what I wanted."[6]

As well, Glyde's style derived elements from English Romanesque art. In painting, the English style is characterized by a strong linear quality and a shallow picture plane. The events often occur right on the picture plane, giving a frieze-like effect, with little depth indicated. Colour is applied to the outlined drawings, filling the shapes described by the line. The drawing has a nervous energy, giving the work a highly animated quality.

At the college, the study of traditional techniques was emphasized. Glyde became especially interested in the tempera medium and worked on large, decorative paintings on boards up to six feet wide, and on smaller panels between ten and thirty inches wide.

The tempera panels were made of plywood, five or six ply, onto which a gauze was glued. Coats of gesso were applied and hand-polished to a marble-like surface. The image was drawn onto this and sometimes stumped using a perforating tool, or the outline was incised into the surface. Powder colours were ground into the tempera medium. Using the Florentine technique, the paint layers were applied, with the colour progressively built up with hatched strokes, becoming stronger and more luminous with the layering. Often complementary colours were applied over one another, for example, green over red, cool colours over warm, or vice versa. This enlivened the surface in a subtle way.

An early tempera work *Perseus and Andromeda* 1929, completed while at the college, is indicative of the kind of work expected by the school both in its technique as well as its classical subject matter. This painting integrates many of Glyde's interests, sources and influences, and amalgamates much of what he had learned at the college: sensitive drawing, draughtsmanship, and a clear sense of design. The cool and restrained use of colour is an early example of a basic tenet of Glyde's work. The colour is of an even overall tonality, with no discordant contrasts. A pale light infuses the space.

The subject of the painting provided a grand theme for Glyde, a theme with an epic quality. The organization of space using a triangle formed by the tilted axes of the two main figures, provides both a central focus and a firm anchor for the composition. All movement is contained within this structure. The rocky outcrops on either side of the foreground provide a frame through which to view the deep landscape. The distant hill town is typical of those of Tuscany found in Italian Gothic paintings. The setting has a gentle naturalism as seen in paintings by Giotto. The floating quality of the figures with their somewhat insubstantial air is, however, more akin to Duccio than Giotto. Light rhythms flow through the work. Plant forms in the foreground are individually represented and delicately drawn.

Delicacy of drawing is also evident in the portrait of his wife *Hilda* 1931. This refined and poetic classical drawing has a quality of serenity and lightness. The expression of grace in the pale luminous face and the crispness of line bring to mind the paintings of Renaissance artist Botticelli. As well as this classical influence, the fine linear drawing with just a hint of shading is reminiscent of drawings of the contemporary British artist Stanley Spencer, as seen in Spencer's *Portrait of Hilda Spencer* 1928 and *The Swiss Nurse* 1931.

Glyde also credits the work of Spencer as an inspiration for his biblical themes. Spencer was influenced by the Pre-Raphaelites as well as Italian Gothic and Renaissance painting.

Spencer's eccentric, visionary work could be seen around London and Glyde knew it well. While still a student, Glyde painted a resurrection scene closely based on a recent painting by Spencer he had seen at the National Gallery. Glyde's painting *The Resurrection* 1927-28 in gouache was small and not as detailed as Spencer's work.

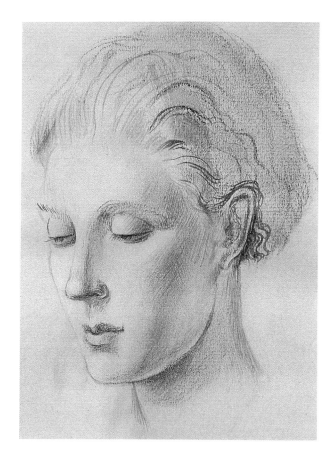

Hilda, 1931
pencil, conté, brush and
Chinese ink on paper
cat. no. 6

The Resurrection, 1927-28
gouache on paper
cat. no. 1

Spencer set his monumental eighteen-foot long *Resurrection in Cookham Churchyard* 1923-26 in a contemporary and local setting, his provincial home town of Cookham. In the same way earlier artists had used their local setting, Glyde stated that Spencer "never got away from the local... Duccio never got away from it. In spite of everything Rubens never got away from it and certainly Rembrandt didn't."[7] However, this was an unusual approach and uncommon amongst other artists of the time. It is remarkable that Glyde became allied to this idea and that it appeared consistently in his future work.

Like Spencer, Glyde set his resurrection in a contemporary churchyard, and it is, similarly, a bird's-eye view. The newly resurrected emerge in a leisurely fashion from open graves. Figures are clustered and, in some cases, compressed together and elongated very much in the manner of Spencer. The space is defined by the back wall of the church and the churchyard wall, providing a relatively shallow space as Spencer did. Two trees, very formal in shape, are more reminiscent of Giotto and Duccio than Spencer, though they are painted in detail, leaf by leaf, as Spencer would have painted them.

Spencer's influence on Glyde is quite specific in this work but it is important in more general terms in Glyde's work as a whole. Some of Glyde's later works have a similar strangeness, partly due to the deliberately awkward compositions, tilting of perspective, and unusual settings.

Though figures by both are conceived as rotund and are solid forms, they can also be flattened and attenuated. Forms are filled out and anatomy simplified for compositional and expressive reasons. Figures may be shown standing or sitting at too pronounced an angle and distorted in a way that gives a queer, awkward effect. Like Spencer, Glyde's close attention to detail was balanced by his imaginative inventiveness.

A tempera painting by Glyde which integrates many of his early influences is *Country Dance* 1935. In this well balanced, logical composition the setting is still classical, though it appears more like the rolling hills of England than an Italian hill town. The activity of the figures is again enacted in a shallow foreground space. What is new here is the originality and the liveliness of the scene. It has the immediacy of an event known and understood and the image carries this conviction. The figures are robust and filled with energy. Rhythm flows through the forms and drapery of the figures, from the dancing group, to the players, to the onlookers.

Colour in this painting is restrained and there is a very careful balance of tonal values. Glyde was not a colourist. He had little training in this area and much of the work he admired was monochromatic. He had no experience of using colour expressively or of incorporating bold juxtapositions of colour as many modernist painters did. His understanding of colour was as an adjunct of drawing,

Perseus and Andromeda, 1929
egg tempera on gesso panel
cat. no. 3

to complement drawing by the application of close tonal values. With these restrictions he used delicate colour sensitively.

Glyde exhibited with the Royal Academy in London between 1931 and 1933. The Royal Academy remained the bastion of conservatism.[8] In the 1920s and early 1930s, the Academy was respected for organizing important exhibitions of Old Masters. In 1930 *Italian Art A.D. 1200-1900* must have been of particular interest to Glyde. This exhibition points to a pervasive British interest in Italian Art. Roger Fry was lecturing and publishing on the subject. His essays, *Giotto* and *The Art of Florence*, were included in *Vision and Design*, first published in 1920. Botticelli was particularly influential. Interest in Italian art was embedded in British art.

Partly through this influence, the human figure regained its traditional pre-eminence.[9] As well, England had a distinguished group of portrait painters in the 1920s. Art critic of the time, Frank Rutter said:

"In new inventions in paint, in the evolving of new styles, new manners and new theories of art, England plainly could not hold a candle to France. But in plain, honest portraiture... it could be done in England... better than anywhere else."[10]

Glyde's art developed in this milieu of conservative British art of the 1920s and reflected the pervasive interest in the figure. In the 1920s even the most advanced group of painters, affiliated with the London Group and the 7 & 5 Society, moved away from radical styles. There was a general tendency away from abstraction. Roger Fry, a member of the London Group, noted a renewed interest in British art, in vigorously planned construction, an increased coherence of design, and sympathetic treatment of architectural subjects, which pointed to these more conservative concerns.

Glyde had little contact with modernist concerns developed in France or advances made in England in the 1930s after the formation in 1933 of Unit One. This group was truly contemporary in spirit, with concerns tending towards abstraction. It included Paul Nash, Ben Nicholson, Edward Burra, Edward Wadsworth, Barbara Hepworth, and Henry Moore. Herbert Read was their spokesman. These artists showed greater pre-occupation with surface texture, the sovereignty of colour and shape, and non-representational forms. Glyde's work was firmly rooted in the academic tradition with an emphasis on naturalism and imagery. His drawing and representational studies were based on the figure. Neither the man nor his art was flamboyant; his work had a firm logical structure. He had already shown his ability and sensitivity as a draughtsman and designer, and had a good grasp of various techniques. He well understood the language of form and through his classical training, could compose harmonious, well designed figurative compositions.

Some of the members of Unit One also produced work which was simplified and logical in structure. But they were concerned with formal values, and the simplification tended towards pure abstraction. By the mid-1930s, for instance, Ben Nicholson was producing sculptural reliefs with an extremely shallow depth based on the circle, square, and rectangle.

Another new mode of expression was surrealism. Though the first International Surrealist Exhibition was not staged in London until 1936, there were elements of the style in England before that. The imaginative aspects of the style appealed to English artists. Edward Wadsworth, another member of Unit One, painted still lifes and seascapes in which disassociated objects were incongruously juxtaposed in a surreal manner.

At this time Glyde's art showed no kinship with these tendencies. His art removed him from the new generation of independent avant-garde painters affiliated with Unit One. In a way, he was caught between the energy prior to World War One, spearheaded by Roger Fry and the New English Art Club when England began to absorb the advances of French art, and the new developments in the late 1930s stimulated by the arrival of refugee artists from Europe.

Glyde's interest in murals was also related to conservative ideas. There had been a revival of interest in mural painting in England in the early 20th century from the time of Frank Brangwyn's brilliantly coloured panels for Skinner's Hall completed in 1909. Gradually other artists undertook commissions for mural decoration. Work in the French tradition of Puvis de Chavannes was carried out in England by F. Cayley Robinson. In the 1910s, artists who decorated St. Stephen's Hall in the Houses of Parliament in Westminster included George Clausen, Walter Monnington, William Rothenstein, and A.K. Lawrence. Young artists from the Borough Polytechnic were involved by Roger Fry in an interesting mural project.[11] Rex Whistler, newly graduated from the Slade, decorated the Refreshment Room at the Tate Gallery in 1926 and 1927. By the 1920s, there had been an increase in demand for murals for public buildings and private dwellings. This stimulated interest in the schools. Of great significance from 1926 were Spencer's murals for Burghclere Chapel completed in 1932.[12]

While Glyde was still a student at the college the registrar had put him in touch with the mural painter Colin Gill. Gill had been commissioned by the Bank of England to contribute to its series of murals, *The Bank in Being*. He hired Glyde as his assistant on the project.[13] The murals were vigorous and realistic in style, with life-sized monumental figures placed in formal architectural settings. The work was done on wood panels and canvas. Gill worked out the designs and Glyde squared them up and transferred them onto the panels. Glyde worked primarily on historical portraits with architectural scenes of London in the background. He did the drawing in pencil, conté, or Prisma colour, monochromatically establishing the full tonality. Glyde painted some of the backgrounds but Gill painted the portraits and put in all the finishing touches.[14] The painting was executed in tempera and the colour was subdued in a close tonal range.

Glyde has recalled, ''I was just a working assistant for him at that time. But, it was a technical background which was really very, very useful.''[15]

In 1930 Glyde was commissioned to paint dioramas of colonial scenes for the Imperial Institute. In the studios of the Institute, he worked on a number of panels, primarily landscapes with figures seen at a distance, engaged in activities related to the copra, peanut, and other industries. They were highly illustrative; their figures lacked the lively energy which Glyde was developing in other work. Glyde himself was disappointed. He was not particularly interested in the subject.

Despite the fact that commissions provided income, Glyde did not enjoy them. They left him with little time to

Abingdon, Oxfordshire, c.1931
watercolour over conté on paper
cat. no. 5

do his own work. "I found it reasonably satisfactory when I could leave the commerical work alone. I became much more interested in so-called 'easel painting.' And I enjoyed teaching." [16]

Glyde had begun teaching in his final year at the college. He taught one afternoon at the Royal College, in the evening at the Borough Polytechnic, and the Croydon School of Arts and Crafts. In 1931 he began teaching full-time at High Wycombe School of Arts and Crafts.

As well as teaching, Glyde was trying to do his own painting. He tried to send something to the Academy exhibitions each year. "I used to do just enough to get something into the Academy... that was a great disappointment. I didn't do a great deal." [17] He managed to exhibit only one or two paintings at the Academy each year from 1931 to 1933. He also exhibited with the Royal Society of British Artists.

He continued to do landscape painting as he had done since his days at the Brassey Institute, working out-of-doors in watercolour. Whenever he was back in Hastings, he went out painting with his friend Alfred C. Leighton. Leighton was a commerical artist who designed toys and produced brochures and posters for such companies as the Canadian Pacific Railway. They had met about 1923 when Leighton came to the Brassey Institute to do some work in the drawing class where he had earlier studied. For Glyde the painting trips with Leighton were an enjoyable experience.

A Village Church, Sussex, 1929
watercolour over pencil
on paper
cat. no. 4

Leighton's father would drive them into the country where they often spent a full day. Glyde and Leighton worked in a similar style at that time, producing watercolours in the traditional 19th century English style. Glyde favoured towns or architectural structures such as churches or windmills set in landscape. His studies were first carefully drawn, with attention to the architectural details. Harmonious, closely-keyed colour was then applied within the shapes defined by the drawing. Working on a cream-coloured Whatman or David Cox paper, he would build up the colour, painting one colour over another with a fairly dry brush. This treatment limited the freshness associated with the watercolour medium. Dashes of red or orange provided a spark of colour which enlivened the studies.

Some of Glyde's landscapes with their low horizon line and large sky are reminiscent of the pastoral and peaceful rolling landscape of Thomas Girtin (1775-1802). The pencil detailing and the colour of his architectural studies is also comparable with that of Girtin. There are architectural views which recall John Sell Cotman (1782-1842). Cotman painted a watercolour, *Mont St. Michel* in 1818, which has a striking similarity to a work of the same subject by Glyde in the 1920s. Glyde's low toned, almost monochromatic colour, with an emphasis on the blue and brown tonal range, is similar to much 19th century English watercolour painting. Glyde's watercolours at this time, though quite proficient, were not as refined and

accomplished as those of the British artists who inspired him. They lack the romanticism of their more lyrical paintings.

After Glyde went to London, he and Leighton continued to go sketching together in the summertime. Glyde also did some commerical work for Leighton. This included illustrations and booklets for Canadian Pacific.

"I used to come down periodically and do work for him in his studio, Canadian Pacific work. I used to help him on all sorts of things. For instance, the launch of the Duchess of Athol and boats of that kind. There were all kinds of things done with a great deal of calligraphy and then little decorations and illustrations. These things were given to people on the maiden voyage. They were little booklets about this size. And printed. I used to help him out on lots of this stuff. So, I really got to know him very intimately." [18]

Leighton had already visited Canada in 1925 through his work for Canadian Pacific and had brought back many watercolours from that trip which he showed to Glyde. "Watercolours — we used to look through them — I found them quite fascinating." [19] Leighton talked to Glyde about Calgary where Leighton was to begin teaching in 1929. He told Glyde that the city was an excellent place, with much to do for someone with a pioneering spirit. During these talks they also discussed the idea of Glyde going to Canada.

Country Dance, 1935
egg tempera on gesso panel
cat. no. 9

Below Rundle, Canmore, 1951
oil on canvas
cat. no. 54

Dumbarton Rock, 1949
mixed technique, pen and ink
on canvasboard
cat. no. 44

Outskirts of Lethbridge, Alberta, June 1938
watercolour over pencil on paper
cat. no. 14

CANADA • ADVENTURE AND EXPERIENCE

In the spring of 1935, Leighton invited Glyde to come to Canada. Leighton wished to improve the faculty at the Provincial Institute of Technology and Art with a strong drawing instructor. Taking a leave of absence from the High Wycombe School of Art, Glyde agreed to come for a year. He, his wife Hilda, and their young daughter Helen arrived in Calgary on 30 September, 1935. As Glyde recollects, it was a lovely autumn day.

Glyde did not intend to stay. He felt very isolated and missed particularly the cultural amenities available in London. He did not like Calgary; he felt it lacked a sense of permanence and stability. He also had to come to grips with his first Canadian winter, a particularly long and cold one. Despite these drawbacks, he quickly became involved in the artistic life of the city. He began teaching at the Institute alongside Leighton, Jim Dichmont, and Marion MacKay (Nicoll), and he joined the Alberta Society of Artists.

In the spring of 1936, he was invited on a trip to the Rockies with Paul Gishler and Ormond Whitman. Gishler and Whitman hiked while Glyde painted and absorbed the full effect of the spectacular scenery around Lake Louise. He was fascinated by and fell in love with the mountains. The trip convinced him that there was a great deal to explore here, and he decided to stay in Calgary for a few more years.

Reflecting recently on the early years at the Institute, Glyde felt that when he arrived the teaching was sound and the courses well structured. There was a lack of equipment, but Glyde saw little difference between the methods used in Calgary and those at the schools he knew in England. He felt that the early teachers had made an important and worthwhile contribution and had established firm roots for art education in Alberta. However, he did feel that in style, art in Calgary was out-of-date and old-fashioned.

Just after Christmas that first year, Leighton, who had been overworked and under stress, became quite ill. Glyde took over some of his classes, but by the end of the term in 1936, Leighton was still exhausted. He took time off and travelled to England to rest. He did not return to his teaching post in Calgary and officially resigned in 1938. At the request of Dr. Carpenter, principal of the Institute, Glyde took over as head of the art department.

In its art courses, the Institute provided an Elementary Diploma, which could be followed by a two-year Advanced Diploma in three categories: Fine Arts, Commerical Art, and Applied Arts and Crafts. As well, there was a one-year teacher's art course offered for students who had completed the Normal School training.

In all courses there was an emphasis on drawing — still life, antique, anatomy, and life drawing. Painting was primarily in watercolour and gouache; oil painting was uncommon. Theory, which involved the History of Art and Art Appreciation, was offered in the elementary course.

Glyde had a full program, teaching both day and evening classes. He taught drawing, design and painting, some block printing, manuscript illustration, and lettering. He demonstrated watercolour techniques and how to paint landscape out of doors. He did not teach the more complex technical processes he had learned as a student in London, such as egg tempera, casein, and other mural processes. Though mural painting was listed for the first time in the 1936-37 prospectus, it seems it was not actually taught. Glyde had not been able to convince Carpenter to support the mural painting course — Carpenter felt it would ruin the walls![1]

While Glyde inherited the structure of the courses, essentially he found it to be consistent with his own training. The emphasis on painting in watercolour was handed on from A.C. Leighton. But it was also a mirror of late depression years in which funds and materials, other than the most basic, were unavailable. Although Glyde did discuss various more complex techniques with his senior students, he did not teach them at the Institute. Furthermore, most art students at the Institute had no prior background in art and Glyde had to establish a basic foundation for them. The more complex mural techniques were not really appropriate to such a course.

Though Glyde did not actually teach Art History, he introduced his students to a wide range of artists. He focused particularly on the Gothic artists, especially Cimabue and Duccio whom he admired so much, as well as British artists. He tried to direct his students to artists who would provide a particular impetus for their work. For example, he introduced Stanford Blodgett to Degas for his fine drawing and to William Orpen for portraiture. However, there was an acute lack of reproductions for him to show the students, which meant they could not absorb the full impact of these lessons.

In his second year at the Institute, Glyde introduced nude models. He encountered opposition from Dr. Carpenter who was afraid of complaints, particularly from the church. Glyde felt strongly that life drawing was an integral part of the course and he ultimately convinced Carpenter to allow the classes to continue.

In his teaching, Glyde emphasized three dimensional form based on classical principles and orderly organization. Despite his interest in depicting the natural world, he was concerned with simplifying forms and finding their essence.

"He talked about making order out of chaos. He emphasized structure. His concept of design was, study the plant or the object, understand the anatomy of it thoroughly. He would go right into the abstract on his design and he would modify, stylize and simplify it."[2]

Glyde developed a growing commitment to the school. In 1939 he stated,

"We feel that this department is fostering a spirit which will make itself felt, in time, throughout Canada. No matter how varied the types of talent that we get, the same vigorous desire for the best and only the best, is manifested in every student."[3]

One of his first students, Stanford Perrott, described Glyde's contribution to the school: "The local scene was stultifying and static; it would have to be an exceptional pioneer or missionary who would come into the atmosphere of the time and make anything of it." Glyde was that pioneer.[4]

In the 1930s and early 1940s, art education in Alberta was just beginning to be established. For students who wished to continue their studies, there was a frustrating lack of local schools and there were no university courses. As Glyde has said, "There was very little locally so the majority of our people went away. There was very little going on in the art field outside of those institutions at all. We had to build up some kind of core."[5] Professional outlets were few also. Students who did not move on to teach generally became commercial artists. Glyde assisted those students who wished to continue their studies or get established elsewhere.

Some of Glyde's important students at this time included Betty Carlisle, Janet Middleton, Luke Lindoe, Stanford Perrott, Stanford Blodgett, Ted Faiers, Margaret Shelton, and Wilfred Beny. All of these students went on to establish significant careers in art for themselves, as teachers and artists.

Glyde's characteristic method of teaching was to demonstrate. He would do rapid drawings on the blackboard, which he quickly erased. These sketches would give students ideas about composition and structure. He also did studies in various materials to demonstrate techniques. He would move amongst the students once they had begun work and make corrections directly onto their work. "He would demonstrate on my paper and it was so exactly right and so feeling!"[6]

Glyde was quite popular with the students and was considered more forthright and sympathetic than his more aloof and withdrawn predecessor, Leighton. Blodgett found him, "Practical, down to earth and direct. I immediately admired the man due to his facility with pen and brush. He taught me design but mostly life drawing. I thought he was a wonderful artist [and] I thought he was an excellent teacher." Blodgett remained Glyde's student for about seven years. "He kept showing me new things all the time."[7]

Glyde supported the idea of originality and an essentially Canadian art. Glyde felt that Tom Thomson was the

Henry Glyde and colleagues at the Banff School of Fine Arts, c.1947
Back Row: A.Y. Jackson, J.W.G. Macdonald
Middle Row: George Pepper, James Dichmont, André Biéler, Murray MacDonald, Marion Nicoll
Front Row: W.J. Phillips, H.G. Glyde

Henry Glyde and students working in the field, c.1945

first man to look at the Canadian landscape with the true eye of a Canadian. He considered him a genius with a goal and great faith in Canada.[8] "The development by western painters of a distinctive style with its own individual characteristics is what we must look forward to if we are going to have a truly realistic and representative art."[9]

In the first years the art department was housed with the rest of the Institute on Calgary's north hill. However, during the war, the Institute buildings were needed by the Air Force for a wireless school. The art department relocated in the Coste House, an old mansion in the Mount Royal district of Calgary. During the war, enrollment included, as usual, students from the Normal School but also military wives and pupils from the Montessori School. The majority of adult students were women. Other teachers joined the staff, including Arthur Adam, Walter Phillips, Marmie Hess, and Jim Dichmont. After the war, the art department returned to the north hill with the rest of the Institute.

An exhibition program was started at Coste House in 1942. Glyde himself had a one-man show there in 1944. But the cultural interests of the school's members extended beyond art into other areas. Glyde, who was involved in both a drama and music group at Coste House, realized the potential for an organization which would unite the arts and provide a venue for events. "For first voicing the idea of an 'Allied Arts' organization rather than a graphic art gallery, the credit goes to Professor H. G. Glyde."[10] This idea was supported by the Calgary Art Association and the Civic Centre Committee.[11]

Once the return of the art school to the north hill became inevitable, Glyde initiated discussions with the mayor, the city librarian Alex Calhoun, and others in connection with establishing an allied arts centre at Coste House. Archie Key was hired as director at the centre. Other members of the executive were Alex Calhoun, Doug Doherty, and Doug Motter. Coste House proceeded to play a central role in the development of the arts in Calgary. After 1949 it became the organizing centre for the Western Canada Art Circuit which circulated exhibitions across the prairies.

Besides the Allied Arts Centre and the Institute, Glyde's other chief area of concern was the Fine Arts School in Banff. In the summer of 1936, Glyde, assisted by Leo Pearson and Nan Lawson Cheney, had taken over Leighton's position as director of the Banff School. The summer art classes had been started by Leighton in 1933 at Seebe and were held there again in 1934. From 1935 they were held in Banff where the art section shared the facilities of the Theatre School under the aegis of the University of Alberta. In 1936 the art, drama, and music administrations were combined under the title of the Banff School of Fine Arts, directed by Donald Cameron.

Banff attracted a varied group of students. As well as students from the Institute in Calgary and later from the University of Alberta, there were some students from other art schools and universities in Canada, for example the Ontario College of Art, and a few students from the United States. There was a core of serious professional students, but the beauty of the environment at Banff also attracted those who wanted to enjoy the pleasures of the area. The students worked primarily in watercolour but some carried canvas boards for oil sketches.

During Glyde's first summer there it was Leo Pearson, drafting instructor at the Institute, who introduced Glyde to Banff, the landscape, and the kind of program Leighton had run the previous summers.

This was Glyde's first experience of this type of teaching. The classes did not have to go far afield to find suitable subjects to paint.

"We stayed close because it all depended upon the number of cars and students. I don't know how many there would be that first year we were there. About thirty or something like that. We stayed pretty close to home. Beyond Banff Avenue, there was the church. There was Wall Street and very interesting houses along the Echo River and places like that." [12]

In later years, students also drove to Bow Falls, Castle Mountain, and Sundance Canyon. Most of the classes were held out of doors. It was only rainy days that kept them indoors.

As the school developed, Glyde became more involved. "Glyde was in his element in Banff. All the time there were cultural things going on and we went to plays and there were choral and speech evenings and there were new writers in Alberta who were producing things and he was keen about that." [13] In Banff in the early years, the Glyde's lived in one of Catherine Whyte's houses. Later they rented their own large house near the Cave and Basin.

Over the years, different artists were brought in to teach with Glyde in Banff, initially only one or two per summer. In 1938 Bernard Middleton, and the following year Middleton and John McLellan, both from Calgary, assisted. From 1940, well known artists came from eastern Canada: André Biéler and Walter J. Phillips in 1940, Charles Comfort in 1941, George Pepper in 1942, and A.Y. Jackson in 1943. After the war, enrollment increased dramatically, and up to a dozen teachers were needed each summer. From 1948, Banff started inviting artists from other countries: Frederic Taubes of New York from 1948 to 1950, Edward Bawden from England in 1949 and 1950, and William Townsend from England in 1951. The core of local teachers centred around Glyde provided continuity for the school.

This balance provided a lively and broad based teaching body for the school, and a very rich environment for the students. It undeniably made an important contribution to the growth and maturity of the art community in Alberta.

Glyde joined the Alberta Society of Artists (A.S.A.) in November 1935. Their regular weekly meetings were a good gathering place for artists and Glyde met many local artists through the Society.

At the time Glyde joined, there had been some controversy about the lessons that Leighton insisted all members should attend. Leighton had stipulated that if they did not, they would lose their membership. He had resigned briefly that year as a means of getting members to agree to the lessons. Some of the members resigned in protest. When Leighton left Calgary, Glyde took over his duties as president, though he had not been elected to the position. Glyde felt he was standing in for Leighton but he remained acting president until 1947. He was also elected to a short term as chairman in the late 1930s. Glyde continued the Thursday classes and criticism though there was a fairly small group still interested. He also organized juries from the membership for exhibitions and sometimes acted as juror himself. As he was involved in the jury, he exhibited little with the Society. [14] Exhibitions were held in the Herald building, the old courthouse, the library, the Institute, and at the Stampede.

Glyde became increasingly less active with the A.S.A. and, after his move to Edmonton, was very little involved. This incurred some resentment among other members. "People in the A.S.A. accused him of being on the executive and playing no part in it, and there was some bitterness." However, Perrott points out that the A.S.A. "was a totally desperate organization, always on the point of collapsing." [15]

In the early 1950s Glyde stopped exhibiting with the A.S.A. He was tired of the arguments and conflicts amongst members and found the atmosphere within the group unpleasant.

In 1940 Glyde met Jack and Grace Turner who had just arrived in Calgary from Edmonton. They became close friends and the Turners visited the Glydes in Banff where, through Geo, they met many artists including Pepper, Jackson, Biéler, and Phillips. Jack occasionally went on sketching trips with Glyde. In 1945 the Turners realized a long held desire to establish a commercial art gallery in Calgary. Glyde, Jackson, and Phillips gave them paintings to start up with, which they sold on consignment. Grace Turner has said: "The initial encouragement of Mr. Glyde and the connection with the Banff School opened many doors." [16]

The Canadian Art Galleries, the first commercial gallery in Calgary, provided important encouragement

Sketching Group, c.1942
watercolour and gouache
on paper
cat. no. 24

and support for Calgary artists. Though the emphasis was on local artists, Canadian Art Galleries also showed the work of other important Canadian artists, including Jackson, Biéler, Pepper, and Lilias Torrance Newton.[17] Besides exhibiting work, the gallery also supplied artists' materials.

As their first gallery at 332 Seventh Avenue S.W. was small, the Turners held the first large one-man exhibition of Glyde's work at Coste House in March 1946, showing one hundred works. The exhibition opened with a tea on a Sunday afternoon, attended by more than 400 visitors. The reviewer Archie Key stated, "This artist paints with vigor. He is essentially a modernist. His approach is intellectual and his technique is sound. He has feeling for form and mass."[18] Glyde had subsequent exhibitions at Canadian Art Galleries and regularly sent work for sale, and continued to do so after he moved to Edmonton. Glyde showed mainly landscapes of which those in watercolour were the most popular and saleable.

In 1937, Glyde became involved in teaching community classes. Dr. Carpenter of the Institute considered it important to have art teachers going into the smaller rural communities where there was no art instruction available, to provide guidance and encouragement, and develop an appreciation of art in the community. Through the extension department of the University of Alberta, Donald Cameron, in the summer of 1937, arranged the first classes

in Vegreville and Vermilion. Subsequently, Lethbridge, Medicine Hat, Peace River, and other towns were added. Each community established its own group and Glyde would go out to teach them. Glyde initially found it a challenge to teach people with little or no prior training and ultimately found it extremely worthwhile.

He also loved the travelling and the exposure it gave him to the Alberta landscape. "I got a great kick out of it because it made me see the country."[19]

The first class in Vegreville was organized by Laura Evans Reid:

"Mrs. Reid, a doctor's wife, organized a very enthusiastic group of housewives, teachers, and others and classes were held three days a week for a month, first in a small church basement crowded with all sorts of things, later in a schoolroom. Lectures and demonstrations were given during the evening and outdoor classes were held during the day. The alternate three days were spent at Vermilion, a further sixty miles east of Vegreville."[20]

Reid herself was extremely talented and had a vivid imagination: "Always she exhibited something which was original and indigenous of this country. Not bound by academic rules, she painted as her spirit moved her; her sketches were painted in a technique which was the envy of all those hampered by the orthodox approach."[21]

For the first six years Glyde taught all the classes and up to 1945 his only other assistant was Phillips. Subsequently, other teachers, including Annora Brown,

The Three Sisters, 1936
watercolour over pencil
on paper
cat. no. 11

Florence Mortimer, Murray MacDonald, Marion Nicoll, and Jack Taylor became involved and a network of classes was set up. Young graduates of the Institute and the University of Alberta benefited from the work it provided and the communities were enriched by a diverse and enthusiastic group of teachers. An important result of the courses was that an art club was usually formed in each town.

Glyde's involvement in the community art classes was unusual; it indicated a populist approach to education. Alison Forbes pays tribute to this approach: "He was not a Canadian yet he wanted to go out and teach art to those people. He took it on with great zest and enthusiasm. He felt that that would eventually give Alberta a sensitivity to Fine Art. We were really fortunate to have a guy like that." [22] Until the early 1950s Glyde remained the teacher most consistently involved in the program.

Henry Glyde with members of
the Medicine Hat Art Club,
late 1930s

CONSOLIDATION • EARLY WORK IN CALGARY

Glyde arrived in Canada a well trained academic painter with superb drawing skills and a strong sense of composition. His response to his new environment and the influence of people he met here was profound. It is to his credit that he absorbed and incorporated these influences in his work, yet retained the essential elements already established in England.

His early work here increasingly showed the effect of this environment. His teaching in Banff and in the extension classes soon after his arrival provided an excellent opportunity to get to know the character of the country: the mountains, foothills, and prairies. The physical charm of the landscape held his interest and he responded quickly to the varied terrain. Landscape studies he did in the field at this time were small and initially only in watercolour. He continued his English method using the drawing to set the composition, then filling it in with subdued colour washes in a brown to blue tonal range. Increasingly, however, there was less detail in the work and no overpainting. The paint was applied in broad washes with more fluid brush work and was thereby lighter, which, in combination with a whiter paper, provided an airy transparent appearance. These were fresh, outdoor sketches, different from the dry and layered English watercolours. The naturalism of these paintings is the result of direct and careful observation. Scenes are observed and quickly rendered, distilling the essence of the landscape. They are depictions of nature in a quiet and subdued state and relate closely to Glyde's approach as a classicist — to show the appearance of things in a calm and studied way. It is nature tamed, a settled rural Alberta. There are no tumultuous scenes of nature in conflict, storms, wind-lashed prairies or blizzard-racked mountains, or even the bursting growth of nature as a romantic may have chosen to depict the region.

Generally Glyde retained the low horizon line of his earlier work and his interest in architecture set in landscape. As seen in *Vegreville Skyline* 1937, grain elevators and barns replaced the earlier churches and windmills of England as subjects within the landscape. He also more frequently depicted pure landscape, devoid of man's works. He felt that the nearby mountains, with their monumentality and solidity of form, provided a parallel for the architectural structures. "I got back into the mountains and I was back into architecture. There's something eternal about them."[1]

In *The Three Sisters* 1936, using a simplified linear structure he shows the massive forms of the mountains. Thin washes of colour have been applied, giving a fresh airy quality.

By the late 1930s, as seen in *Outskirts of Lethbridge, Alberta* 1938, Glyde's watercolours had attained a simplicity of treatment and a lightness which made them sparkle. This watercolour has a liveliness not seen in the English works. The tonal range is broader and brighter colour has been used. Though drawing still provides the structure, it

The River Bottom, 1938
watercolour over conté on paper
cat. no. 15

is less evident and there is a stronger emphasis on the paint quality and surface. Another change has appeared in the raising of the horizon line to the upper third of the composition.

An interesting feature of these early Canadian watercolours is the increasing rhythm in the work. Though this was evident in the English watercolours, it was not obvious. In *The River Bottom* 1938, which depicts the dry, undulating prairie, there is a sweep of rhythm from the foreground which flows into the middle distance. To Glyde, the prairies "reminded me of an ocean, there was never a straight line. My horizons got quite high so that I could put movement on the prairie itself. It struck me as being full of movement."[2]

Though Glyde responded to the Alberta landscape, he continued to paint compositions using the figure. Soon after his arrival in Canada, he painted *Skaters*. Unlike earlier large compositions which he painted in tempera, this is painted in oil. Oil is more transparent than tempera and provided a luminosity to this work not seen in the earlier paintings.

The snow in this painting is shown in clumps, making rounded forms which join in gentle, undulating rhythms. This stylization, the simplification of forms into rhythms, was an aspect of Glyde's work which would become more pronounced in the 1940s under the influence of A.Y. Jackson. It is already clearly evident in this earlier work.

Skaters shows loose groups of people huddled together in the snow in the river valley in Calgary, with skaters in the middle distance and a cabin to the right. The heavily clothed figures are drawn as solid shapes, the forms of the bodies extremely simplified and expressed as volumes. Each knot of figures is self-contained but is linked with the next in a rhythmic flow. The grouping relates to Italian influences long absorbed, of artists such as Giotto, whose massed groups of figures are linked with strong internal movement. A thin brown line delineating the figures gives an overall unity. This device was an inherent characteristic of Glyde's work and appears in most of his figure compositions.

The grouping of figures with connecting rhythms is taken up again in the watercolour *Lunch, Vegreville* 1938. The stylized, carefully modelled, though attenuated and somewhat flattened figures recall Stanley Spencer in their awkwardness and oddnesss. In its rustic setting with ordinary folk enjoying the fruits of the harvest and in its implicit affirmation of rural life, this painting is related in theme to the American Regionalists.

Glyde's work has sometimes been termed Regionalist. The Regionalist movement of the 1920s and 1930s was one in which American artists defined national identity in landscape and genre painting with a native subject matter. Set in the mid-west, it advocated the perpetuation of an agrarian over urban society. Democratic in intent, the

Lunch, Vegreville, 1938
watercolour over pencil
on paper
cat. no. 13

Skaters, 1935-36
oil on canvas
cat. no. 10

The Music Group, 1940s
oil on canvas
cat. no. 20

realism of the work was meant to facilitate communication with the broad American middle-class whom the Regionalists represented in their paintings. The three major Regionalists were Thomas Hart Benton, John Steuart Curry, and Grant Wood. The movement was eclipsed in the 1940s by the international modernist styles developing in New York.

Most of Glyde's work is clearly beyond the time frame of the movement and the political framework of the Depression which stimulated it. His art is not really associated with a national consciousness in Canada. But Glyde is concerned with a commitment to his region, that is of Alberta, which as a primarily rural community provided subjects akin to those of the Regionalists. As with the Regionalists, Glyde represents an aspect of the Canadian environment. Using the locale of Alberta he depicts an idyllic semi-agrarian life with frolicking maidens and lads. He celebrates the countryside and life style of rural Alberta.

Intimacy with place was important to Glyde. He spent much of his time studying the Alberta locale:

"I think since those days I've been able to come to grips with the landscape and people. It wasn't long after [arriving here] that I was drawing cowboys sitting on fences and things of that kind. I spent a long time up in Canmore, year after year, for about six years after Banff. We were going to a cabin and the kids would play in the canyon and I would paint around that same place for about ten days and try to soak it up. I tried as much as I could to get that feeling."[3]

Stylistically his work had much in common with the Regionalist painters. It was representational and, like Benton and Wood, was based on early European painting. His work was formally and logically structured like Wood's, but without the naivety. Like Benton, he painted murals, restaged biblical scenes in a contemporary rural setting, and worked in egg tempera. He often stylized his figures as Benton did, though they did not have the excessive energy of Benton's, nor the brilliant colour.

However, despite these similarities, Glyde's mannered figures stem from this early interest in Romanesque and Gothic art, and, as well, show a clearer relationship to the work of Stanley Spencer, than they do to a Regionalist influence.

Glyde had met Benton in 1941 at the Kingston Conference and knew his work through publications.

"I used to like the genre paintings very much. I was convinced that he knew the people and how they ticked. I knew that he modelled nearly all his stuff and played with light on it. It had a very beautiful rhythm to it."[4]

Glyde's figure painting *The Music Group* 1940s, has a strong Regionalist feeling. The robust, well-formed, mannered figures represent the idealized cowboy-farmer type Glyde often uses in his work. The bright colours of this work, blue, red, and yellow, are characteristic of Benton's colours. The subdued mood conveys a feeling of the peace and security of rural life, and symbolically affirms it.

Prairie Woman, c.1944
oil on canvas
cat. no. 38

Moving In, 1941-42
oil on canvas
cat. no. 23

While Glyde may have been partly influenced by the Regionalists, it is clear that many of his paintings in this period are a continuation of visual ideas developed in *Perseus and Andromeda* and *Country Dance* in England. The idea of the mural as a vehicle for epic themes was a notion carried over into his easel paintings of the 1940s. In 1940 Glyde began a series of major classical compositions in which the figure is a dominant element. These substantial works, though often based on a local theme, have an archetypal quality, transcending the present in time and place. Some of them derive from biblical themes, for example: *The Exodus, She Sat Upon A Hill Above the City, Peace,* and *The Aftermath.* Many incorporate ideas from an interior world of images, from the subconscious, or from the imagination, which are organized into a coherent compositional structure.

Prairie Woman c.1944 is a painting of Glyde's wife Hilda. She is posed in front of a prairie town complete with its grain elevators and barns and set against the mountains, painted in cool, gently graded tones of yellow, green, and blue. Despite the specifics of the figure and landscape, this is not simply a portrait. There is a sense that this woman represents all women, that her acceptance of the condition of life is universal and timeless. A mood of pessimism pervades the work. We are made aware of the loneliness of life in this thinly settled country. F.M. Norbury reviewed this painting amongst others and commented on the "archaic rendering of the subject, which while seeming unrealistic in

modern phrase is yet that more real because it tells of what is perennial in human experience."[5] Compositionally, this painting draws on assimilated classical ideas. The slight twist of the body, the tilt of the head and the downcast eyes are reminiscent of the classical conventions of Italian Madonnas, particularly those used by Leonardo in the *Madonna of the Rocks*; the setting and proportions of the figure to landscape recall the *Mona Lisa.*

Glyde has brought the idea up to date and provided an Alberta setting for what, nevertheless, remains an archetypal subject.

*"There's a chinook arch in the air which I used a great deal as a sense of hope. I think at that time I was looking at Grant Wood. During this period of the forties, I was very interested in Roosevelt's attitude as a result of his public works administration projects. I must say that I saw, at that time, quite a few things done. Grant Wood, and two or three others at that period seemed to fit in with what I was thinking about.''[6]

Prairie Woman has the symbolism of Wood's work without the precision, coldness, and ornateness. It is more expressive and evokes the stark reality of the desolation of the prairies.

Another painting, *Manoeuvres* 1943 has a classical calm and stillness but without any particular classical references. Bathed in the early morning light it has an eerie quiet. The organic, rolling landscape falls away behind the houses, then rises up to distant hills. The simple architecture of the houses is monumental in feeling. Soldiers in the fore-

Manoeuvres
(Currie Barracks Road), 1943
oil on canvas
cat. no. 25

ground hide in the gardens while local residents walk unknowing and unconcerned in the suburban street. Glyde described the scene thus:

"One day I came out of the house and I was going to work. It was about eight o'clock in the morning and I walked quite often to the Coste House. That's where the art school was then. I went out there one morning and I nearly tripped over a fellow in khaki. It was a coldish morning. I think it was October. They just went in and did their little bit of manoeuvering. Straight away I thought there was a composition right there. These houses on the hill just a little way away and that's how that happened."[7]

Despite the fact that this relates to a particular event, this painting too has a generalized epic quality.

Manoeuvres has a dramatic, sparkling light — a long prairie light coming from low on the horizon which spreads across the surface of the buildings giving sharp highlights where it touches, and a reflected light casting warm, glowing shadows. It provides an unreal and theatrical glow, a typical light in Calgary under the Chinook arch. In this diffused, low light, volumes are more clearly modelled. There are brilliant light tones but no dark shadows. The Italian Gothic artists also used that low light.

"I've always been interested in the long shadow, the long light which will give you almost equal darkness from the top of the head to the foot. You get more reflected light of course in your shades with the low light. Fifteenth century people, they have a long shadow. They have a low light. In Calgary it's there. It's always there. The low light below the Chinook."[8]

Many of the oils and watercolours that he did in the 1930s and 1940s use that really low light which washes across the surface.

Where the light illuminates the surface of the buildings, the paint is thick with a scumbled texture. The rest is thinly painted, the colour sparkles, and the paint has a luminous, crisp quality. The whole composition is serene and harmonious, and in perfect balance.

Kluane Lake on Alaska Highway, 1949
oil on canvas
cat. no. 47

THE YUKON TRIP

In 1941 Glyde received a travelling fellowship to attend the Kingston Conference as a representative for artists in Alberta. Organized by André Biéler at Queen's University, the conference brought artists from across Canada together for the first time to meet and discuss issues in the arts. It was the first time Glyde had been east and he met many of the Canadian artists with whose work he was already familiar, particularly members of the Group of Seven. Glyde had seen exhibitions of Canadian art in Calgary which had been toured across the country by the National Gallery in Ottawa.

In Toronto, en route to the conference, Glyde met A.Y. Jackson for the first time at the Arts and Letters Club. Glyde travelled to Kingston with Jackson and sculptors Florence Wyle and Frances Loring. This was the start of a long friendship between Glyde, then in his thirties and the more senior Jackson, nearing sixty. Of the Group, Glyde liked Jackson's work most, though he did think Lismer's work was superb and much underrated. Jackson suggested to Glyde that he abandon his classical themes based on the figure and paint the Canadian landscape. "He helped me to see the landscape without people."[1] Though Glyde followed Jackson's advice about the landscape, he fortunately did not abandon his figurative work.

Glyde was to get to know Jackson even better at the Banff School in the summer of 1943, when Jackson replaced George Pepper, who enlisted and went overseas. In October 1943, Glyde and Jackson went on a trip to the Yukon to make studies of the building of the Alaska Highway, the Canol project, and R.C.A.F. activities, for the National Gallery of Canada. The director of the gallery, Harry McCurry, made the arrangements for them to go north. McCurry had written to G.M. Brown, director of public relations, R.C.A.F., that "we are anxious to make arrangements for two of the country's most competent and well-known artists to go up the Alaska highway... to make a permanent record of the project."[2]

The highway, passing through northern British Columbia and the Yukon, provided a vital Allied defence link. It took considerable time to arrange the necessary permits and authority to sketch along the highway. Furthermore, Glyde had difficulty getting time off from the Institute. Donald Cameron interceded with the Principal, J. Fowler, to release him from his teaching duties as he felt Glyde deserved the recognition that such a commission would give him.[3]

Finally, on 14 October, Glyde and Jackson were ready to leave and arrived at Whitehorse by transport plane. On seeing the terrain both men realized that it would take all their time to record the American Army Corps of Engineers at work on the highway. They were driven west to Kluane Lake, near the Alaska border, and then returned to Whitehorse. From there, with only a week, they undertook the 850-mile journey southeast to

Dawson Creek, where the new road joined the old road to Edmonton. When they reached Fort St. John just north of Dawson Creek they were to return by plane to Edmonton. Their hosts, the U.S. Army, facilitated their travel and accommodation along the highway. As Glyde wrote to McCurry:

"Major Vann Kenney of The North Western Command was a gem. He spent considerable effort in arranging the whole expedition enabling us to get the most out of our time.

"The P.R.A. [Public Roads Administration] under Mr. Andrews at Whitehorse was also extremely helpful. They furnished us with car and driver."[4]

Glyde and Jackson worked their way down the road recording the landscape and men at work on the highway and in the camps. In many places they stopped only briefly for fifteen minutes to make sketches, due to the extensive country they had to cover and record. This was an important trip for Glyde. He had never been in a place which was so wild or so remote. He was intrigued by the way trees and plants clung to life. He felt there was a special quality of light. Jackson described the impressive terrain:

"We had heard stories about this part of the country, that it was just a great stretch of monotonous bush. Perhaps it was the crisp October weather with the low sun, the sombre richness of the colour, the frost and patches of snow, the ice along the edge of the rivers, but whatever the reason, we found it fascinating."[5]

"For a hundred and fifty miles the road runs through a high open country with mountain ranges on either side. The timber line gets lower in the north so that the mountains rise from the wooded plains with hardly a tree on them. Mile after mile of sharp pointed peaks covered with snow form a background, while the road follows the long swinging undulations of open, wooded country — stretches of spruce and poplar, grassland or burnt-over country, lands of little sticks. There was no snow in the valleys, but the ground was rich with hoar frost where the sun could not find it."[6]

Out in the field, Glyde's sketches were mainly in pencil, to which notes about colour and tone were added. Watercolours and oil paints could not be used out-of-doors as it was too cold. In the evenings, Jackson and Glyde worked up some of the day's drawings on oil panels. As Glyde relates,

"We stayed together in an American camp so that in the evenings, he would often paint on his bed. He'd put up his sketchbox and his panel and work from this pencil sketches and I did that too. It hadn't occurred to me to do that before. I got into the habit of doing it and I do it now."[7]

Glyde did many pencil sketches depicting particularly the work along the highway and the activity within the camps. In these, the salient details are recorded with a quick sure line, some rapid shading, and notes about colour. In *Alaska Highway* 1943, the study for *Bridge Building*, the structure is clearly recorded in a quick sketch. The subsequent oil sketches are carefully structured with details blocked in. They relate closely to the drawings and have a linear, architectural quality. The six oil sketches which were sent to the National Gallery after the trip, including *Bridge Building*, have heavily outlined shapes, with the activities related to construction in the foreground and the background landscape rendered simply. Though some of the outlines are rounded, there are not the emphatic rhythms found in the later finished works.

In Glyde's work from the trip, there is little pure landscape. He carried with him his interest of man in nature. Generally he shows the activity of the workers on the highway, with the sweep of the impressive landscape serving as a backdrop. Along the highway he shows the clearing of the land, road building, bridge building; in the towns he shows supplies being unloaded, arrival of planes, storage sheds; in the camps he depicts men huddled around fires gathering to commence work and relaxing in the bunkhouses. Glyde said:

"I was very interested in some of the things these men did. In the morning, when it was not yet light their hot breath would be coming out forming a fog and there they were struggling with those engines. Well, some of them, I believe, would put the fires on them to warm them up. It was very, very cold at night. And then they'd start up and never stop."[8]

The prevalence of men in the landscape shown in the foreground of the composition distinguished Glyde's work from Jackson's, in which the emphasis is on the landscape, sometimes including diminutive figures. Glyde has remarked that when Jackson did occasionally include figures, they were small and awkward and set in the distance. Jackson deals with open vistas, Glyde's views are generally more contained and much of the activity occurs in the foreground, emphasizing the foreground rather than the distant view.

The scenes also show the climate as severe and austere. Outdoors, the men are heavily dressed to combat the fierce weather. When not working, they are huddled in tightly knit groups. The scenes are bathed in the subdued light of the north. Rich autumnal colours, warm reds and browns, contrast with the icy blues of the sky and sharp white of the snow-clad mountains.

After the trip, the drawings and sketches were synthesized into finished watercolour and oil paintings. Thirty oils and watercolours, exhibited first at Coste House, then at the Calgary Stampede in 1944, were highly praised in a review.[9] In these the rhythm in the mountains, cloudy sky,

Bridge Building, c.1943
oil on wood panel
cat. no. 29

and broad open planes is more obvious, and must be attributed in part to the influence of Jackson. There is also a greater stylization of form, for example, in the trees and figures. Smoke from chimneys has been reduced to horizontal bands of rounded forms. Jackson did help him to see the Canadian landscape and interpret it in a different way.

"I drew very differently than he did, and I didn't see the colour in the same way, but when it came to the rhythm and the feeling and rhythm and volume going together, yes, I learned a lot from that... He always sort of finished a rhythm before he put something on the top; there was a finish to that rhythm and up went his line. Rather like a gesture drawing."[10]

In *Kluane Lake on the Alaska Highway* 1949, the stark, snow-covered mountain echoes and thus emphasizes the forms of the figures in the foreground. Animated rhythms flow through the repeated grooves of the mountains weathered by the ages. Diffused light dramatically highlights the mountain in the background. The sparkling white light on this snow-covered mountain is a counterpoint to the deep shadow of the foreground painted in subdued tones of blue, brown, and mauve. In this work, Glyde captures the feeling of the chilling cold of the north.

The influence of an artist of the stature of Jackson was considerable. However, it tended to emphasize and consolidate elements already present in Glyde's work, rather than, as others have suggested, completely redirecting him. Jackson led him to place more emphasis on the Canadian

Kluane, 1943
conté on paper
cat. no. 26

Sunday, Rosebud, Alberta, 1945
watercolour over pencil
on paper
cat. no. 40

experience, to appreciate the breadth of the spectacular natural landscape. However, stylization and rhythms within the composition were already prevalent in Glyde's work.

Under Jackson's influence though, Glyde painted in oils more frequently. Also, it was after this trip that Glyde began to paint small oil panels in the field.

After the trip, Glyde wrote to McCurry:

"We had a marvellous trip and saw some great material but the time was all too short to take advantage of everything. We gathered many notes and sketches and I think got all we could in the short period.

"I am busy working up some of my notes and sketches, they vary from bridge construction and "Bull dozers" in action to scenes on the R.C.A.F. stations — One particular station called Fort Nelson is very interesting; one could be kept busy for a couple of weeks at this airport." [11]

After his return from the Yukon, Glyde gave one of his regular lectures, a "chalk talk," in Calgary. On large sheets of paper, he drew the mountains and lakes of the Yukon rapidly from memory, recalling his adventures. People eagerly grabbed the sheets to keep as he discarded them. [12]

In the fall of 1944, Glyde and Jackson were ready to go up to the Yukon again for the National Gallery. However, there was so much red tape through the R.C.A.F. that they became impatient and decided to go to Rosebud instead. Jackson had passed through this small town northeast of Calgary sixteen years before and had wanted to return. Jackson wrote:

"It was rolling country all cut up with coulees... Glyde and I spent two weeks there, two weeks of lovely weather, wandering about the hills, painting farms and ranches. We stayed at a pleasant little hotel run by a Dutchman and his French Canadian wife; settlers, who came to the hotel from everywhere around, seemed most friendly people." [13]

Glyde's painting *Sunday, Rosebud, Alberta* 1945 is based on the watercolour sketch *Rosebud* 1944, that he painted on this trip. It has lost none of the freshness and spontaneity of the original, though it is more structured, with defined colour contrasts and more stylized and emphatic rhythms. It also has figures of local country folk where the original had none. This work has the strong genre features of rural life found in Benton's work, and the animation and distortion in the figures is not unlike Benton's.

Glyde based a later oil painting on sketches from this trip. *Rosebud, Alberta* 1947, a rustic scene, has the emphatic rhythms of the undulating prairie, extreme stylization, and strong colour found in Jackson's work.

RELOCATION • EDMONTON AND THE UNIVERSITY

Glyde's eleven years in Calgary were critical to his personal development and teaching. He was happy at the Institute and busy; his teaching schedule was over thirty hours a week. "I was busy, trying my darnedest to do things and, incidentally, it has turned out to be the most successful part of my sojourn in the west, in the foothills area." [1]

It was also a fruitful time for him artistically. He had been able to visit many areas of the province which he captured in drawings and sketches in watercolour and oil. He had been working energetically, producing large complex paintings. "I found it a productive period and I never stopped. I was going back to work at all kinds of odd hours and every spare moment I was drawing." [2] He had regular exhibitions in Calgary, including some important solo shows. His work was also shown in eastern Canada at the Royal Canadian Academy and the Ontario Society of Artists. His work was well received, he was considered modern and had established a strong following.

Why then, with all these achievements, did he choose to uproot his family and move to Edmonton in 1946? Though there was clearly some prestige for him in teaching at the university, there was no existing program. It was to be Glyde's job to set one up and it was not likely that he would be allowed to establish a Fine Arts degree program for some time. There were few universities in Canada with Fine Arts programs. Glyde acknowledges that he went "knowing full well that there wouldn't be a full-time art school at the university. It would be a service department as much as anything." [3] In fact, the Fine Arts degree program was not established at the University of Alberta until 1968.

Perhaps part of the reason was Glyde's frustration that the art department in Calgary, having experienced partial autonomy and involvement with the other arts while at the Coste House during the war, was to return to the large Institute campus in 1946. Dr. Newton noted after a meeting with Glyde and Phillips in Calgary, "They are unhappy in association with Technology. Would like to stay in Coste House. It is becoming a civic art centre." [4]

Glyde also had strong feelings about having an art program available in Alberta at a university level. As he said: "Something's got to be done about our art school people because, at the moment, they move out of the art school without any qualifications at all. That's not fair after four years." He felt the diploma wasn't worth the paper it was written on. "They couldn't get teaching positions anywhere because they didn't have degrees, they only had diplomas." [5]

There had been some discussions at this time about the art department in Calgary becoming affiliated with a university program. Glyde was the only one who supported this and he was considered a traitor by those who feared that if there was a separate art school it would split the Institute.

Glyde had already had substantial contacts with the University before 1946. He had known many of the teachers since 1936 when Dr. Carpenter had taken him to Edmonton to acquaint him with the situation there. From 1937 he had been involved with the Extension Department based in Edmonton and he had taught extension classes in Edmonton from 1943. As early as November 1944, R.W. Hedley of the Edmonton Museum of Arts made a proposal to Cameron to get Glyde on the University staff on a half-time basis.[6] In April 1945, Glyde was appointed to a committee to assist the University in building up a Department of Fine Arts.[7]

It was anticipated that at the beginning, the new department would be mainly concerned with extension work. In May 1945, the committee recommended that a practical art course be set up. This was to include art appreciation, drawing, painting, design and composition, industrial art, stage design, and costume.[8] Finding space for such classes was initially a problem. But in any case, for the fall session of 1945, Glyde could not teach more than the Saturday afternoon and evening classes in Edmonton.[9] By the late summer there was discussion of him working full-time at the University of Alberta.[10]

Glyde was appointed to begin in the fall of 1946. He was offered a house owned by the University and later, in 1949, moved to a university house on campus. This was given in recognition of the excellent service Glyde had already rendered the University on a part-time basis.[11] In Edmonton Glyde had an office at the University which he could use as a studio. In Calgary, the school had not provided a studio, which had necessitated that he work at home. "Donald Cameron gave me an office in the Extension Department and I had one chair and no library and no students — nothing at all."[12] Glyde moved permanently to Edmonton in mid-1946 to begin setting up the art department there. He was pleased that J.W.G. Macdonald, a strong individual with a very good background, would succeed him in Calgary.

In the first year, Glyde had a light teaching load with two classes — drawing and art history.[13] Besides students from the Education Department, there were some from the general B.A. course, the extension classes and a few special students. Notable students enrolled this first year were Alison Forbes, Marcel Asquin, Robert Willis, and Ted Kemp. A library was established and slides gathered for teaching. Cameron was very helpful. The classes were held in the arts building in a room on the top floor. Glyde also taught some extension classes and further developed that program.

In the following year, Jack Taylor came in to assist Glyde as Lecturer in Art and a design course was added.

Jack Taylor was also given responsibility for teaching Art History. Glyde did not enjoy teaching History of Art, "I'd much sooner be in the studio and talking to people. Art History, to me, being something that I used as an aid to this other business of studio work."[14]

What Glyde wanted to do at the University was set up a full-time diploma program modelled on the Slade School in London, a department of the University College, which he had studied on his visit to England in 1949. "I thought we could do something similar here, so that we'd have a full-time diploma."[15]

He didn't expect to establish the diploma program immediately. For the first few years, he planned to build a nucleus of art students. He felt students needed to be prepared and get a few years experience before they entered a diploma program, which in turn he felt would be a good basis for going on to a degree. "There was not enough background for a person to go through with a degree without a diploma."[16] His plans extended beyond the students enrolled at the University. He made the proposal to President Newton in May of 1950, "whereby the better students now attending our numerous Extension and Community Classes in Art could pursue their work to the Diploma status."[17]

In 1953, the first full four-year Diploma Program in Art was established, taught by Glyde and Taylor. It included Fundamentals of Drawing and Painting, Art History and Appreciation, Pictorial Composition, and Advanced Drawing and Painting. Art courses continued to be offered in the Faculty of Education and in the general three-year B.A. program.

In the first year there were four students in the Diploma course. Glyde instilled a strong sense of dedication in his first full-time art students in Edmonton. One of them, Colleen Millard, recalls:

"He was a disciplinarian as far as teaching methods were concerned, building one skill on another and would have preferred that we had painted twenty hours a day and spent the other four in the library. He was an example of that dedication which was hard to emulate. He would draw at lunch time rather than go out to lunch, he would draw after work."[18]

At the University, Glyde continued the teaching methods he had already established. Drawing was considered an important basic; compositional studies for paintings were worked out ahead of time in a small cartoon. He illustrated profusely with chalk on the board, giving some ideas but erasing them quickly. "The air at times was quite filled with chalk dust."[19]

He would begin a project with general discussion and an appraisal of original works of art. Glyde always went over the assignment in detail, engaging the students in

H.G. Glyde and Gwytha
Evans working on the mural
Alberta History, c.1950

discussion to amplify the topic. Then he would do a demonstration, often based on something in his sketchbook.

"He would very carefully tell us why he was mixing this colour with this colour, why he was applying it in that manner. I realized afterwards that not only was he teaching us his method of painting, but he was giving us brush techniques that I had never seen before."[20]

Students learned to mix their own gesso, tempera, mediums, etc. from basic materials. Glyde would go through the various processes methodically, step by step. Forbes, a student, said,

"I thought it was a great course. I really thought we were getting something and then I understood history better. When I went to the States [to continue my studies] they were taking courses in advanced painting. You could do just what you wanted. They didn't even suggest technique or method or subject."[21]

He taught students to develop chiaroscuro, by modelling forms and building up tones with progressive cross-hatching. Finally colour in a limited range was added, and was secondary to the tonal work. He taught his advanced students a variety of painting techniques that he had not taught in Calgary: various ways to paint in watercolour, oil, casein, mixed media, and egg tempera.

Glyde assigned many projects emphasizing the use of the figure. He taught the human figure in terms of volumetric shapes. The head would be an egg, the chest a box, the spine a concertina, and the pelvis would be a wedge. This was an important teaching device to assist in the understanding and representation of volume. The students also studied bone and muscle structure in an anatomy class. In these projects, landscape was not used for its own sake. It provided a background for a figurative composition. "He had a very humanistic interest in subject matter."[22] He sent his students out into the city, into bars and restaurants, to draw from life for projects. He also encouraged his students to go out in the field and work from nature. He expected a truth to nature though without slavishly copying it.

Glyde taught in a very flowing style. In his discussions and teaching, he was animated, striding around the room, posing expressively and using his own body to explain things. As Forbes recalls, in his demonstrations the students were often transfixed by the skill. "He was naturally enthusiastic and affable. He would get poetic about artists who interested him... [He transmitted a] sense of feeling and higher purpose in art."[23]

He discussed quite a wide range of artists in his classes, generally introducing students to artists from whom they could learn something in particular. One artist he mentioned frequently in these early classes was Benton, whom he considered a painter for the people, making art of commonplace subjects for the common people. He discussed Benton's brilliant use and unusual juxtaposition of colour.

He continued to promote his idea of a truly Canadian art. He spoke of the European interpretation of the Canadian landscape and compared that to painting by Canadian artists, particularly the Group of Seven.

In 1949 Glyde introduced mural painting as an advanced course. He taught mural techniques carefully and in detail. He set projects based on historical topics around the theme of heritage in Alberta. Students were encouraged to look at Benton's mural work and they viewed an important film on him.

Glyde was also clearly thinking of this heritage theme in developing his own mural *Alberta History*. He employed two student technicians, Robert Willis and Gwytha Evans, to assist him. Other students who assisted were Alison Forbes and Marcel Asquin. From initial drawings and sketches, a final cartoon, one-third size, was prepared. Care was taken in the drawings to maintain authenticity in costume, buildings, and other details.

Alberta History was designed for the newly constructed Rutherford Library at the University of Alberta. It was a gift from Glyde. It is over twenty feet long by eight feet high and is set fifteen feet above the floor, over the main entrance doorways of the large reading room on the second floor. It is a composite of scenes and events in Alberta history from the period 1850 to 1870. More than twenty figures are depicted; those in the foreground are life-size. The two major figures are the missionaries Father Lacombe and Reverend John McDougall.

The project, begun in June 1950, took over four months to complete, and was unveiled on 15 May 1951. To undertake the mural, scaffolding was put up. The cartoon was projected onto the wall with lantern slides from which an outline could be drawn onto the plaster surface.

The white plaster base of the mural was applied by the building contractor. The basic outline and some detailing were done in charcoal. Instead of an imprimatura, Prisma coloured pencils were used to establish the tones and modelling. Two colours were used — terra cotta and evergreen. The forms were carefully and realistically modelled. Layers of casein were applied over this, both in thin washes and opaque layers. A final varnish was applied.[24]

The broad, epic composition of *Alberta History* is essentially divided into halves; events surrounding McDougall on the left and those around Lacombe to the right. The two parts are linked by the figure and cart in the centre and a more or less continuous horizon line. The narrative is carried into the background to the fort, churches, and Indian villages. Both the bare-chested Indians and the clothed figures, built up with cross-hatched modelling and layered, luminous colour, have a feeling of solidity and volume. A very close tonal range has been used, primarily greens to yellows, and the mural has an overall pastel effect resembling fresco. There are no sharp discordant contrasts. Foreground details of costume and grass are delicately and carefully rendered. Rhythm flows through the groups of figures and is followed through in the undulating landscape. Despite the rhythms, however, the composition is basically classical and static. This was an ambitious project for Glyde, successfully interpreting the early history of the region in a strong narrative composition.

A subsequent mural, *When All the World was Burned*, completed in September 1952, has a more illustrative quality than *Alberta History*. Its forms are strongly stylized and it is quite two-dimensional and decorative. This four-by-sixteen foot mural was commissioned by Helen Beny Gibson for the Students' Union Building at the University of Alberta.[25] Painted on three masonite panels in casein and wax, it is based on a Cree legend. The two main figures, stylized and shown in profile wearing traditional, heavily decorated costumes, are placed in the centre, in front of a tepee. Tightly knit groups of animals huddle in fear on either side. These figures are contrived and generalized, and some of the animal forms are rendered in crude clichés, giving the whole a somewhat sentimental quality. The patterning of the clothing and the heavy outlines serve to flatten the composition and augment the two-dimensional effect. The overall composition, however, is strong and well balanced, and the simplified broad treatment facilitates a "reading" from a distance. The light but subtle tonal range is fresh and sparkling. The mural has a beautiful lustrous surface.

In 1956 Glyde completed a mural for the Medicine Hat Public Library depicting the history of the western pioneers. An aluminum relief, depicting the history of Alberta, was also installed at Edmonton City Hall. An ambitious project for St. Patrick's Roman Catholic Church in Medicine Hat, the *Fourteen Stations of the Cross*, was completed in 1960.

After his move to Edmonton, Glyde continued exhibiting in Calgary and also in Edmonton. Some of these one-person exhibitions toured the province, others toured in western Canada through the Western Canada Art Circuit. He continued to send work east to the Royal Canadian Academy until 1958.

Before Glyde arrived to teach at the University, regular art exhibitions had been held on the second floor of the Arts building.[26] These were arranged and organized by Professor E.S. Keeping and when Glyde arrived in Edmonton, he assisted Keeping. In 1950 Glyde was appointed Curator of the University of Art Gallery and Museum which was established on the top floor of the

Rutherford building. The Gallery mounted university collection and faculty exhibitions, shows from the Banff collection, and exhibits from various parts of Canada, the United States, Britain, and occasionally Europe. Some of these were obtained through the Western Canada Art Circuit. Glyde also co-ordinated the exhibitions at Banff. The Banff School had established a collection in 1939 which was to be exhibited during the summer session for the benefit of the students.

After his move to Edmonton, Glyde contributed considerable energy and time to various new arts organizations. In 1947 he was the Alberta delegate to the national conference of the Federation of Canadian Artists and the Canadian Arts Council.[27] Glyde was elected vice president and representative of Alberta, of the Canadian Arts Council in 1948. From 1954 to 1956, he was president of the Federation of Canadian Artists and the headquarters of the organization moved to Edmonton.[28]

The Alberta Government established a Provincial Arts Board in 1948 and Glyde was appointed chairman of one of the sub-groups, the Alberta Visual Arts Board.[29] The Board worked in co-operation with the Federation of Canadian Artists to encourage, co-ordinate, and develop art and handicrafts in the province. An important part of its activity was to circulate art exhibitions around the province, primarily of Alberta artists' work, though there were occasionally others. The program complemented that of the Extension Department, and a number of teachers from the Fine Arts Department, including Jack Taylor and Norman Yates, were involved.

Under Glyde's guidance, the board organized and circulated exhibitions on two circuits, northern and southern. In 1950 Glyde made an attempt to get funds so that the board could pay fees to artists contributing to the exhibitions, but this was unsuccessful. A handicraft program was spearheaded and community workshops organized. The Board secured donors who gave money for scholarships for students to attend art school in Calgary, Edmonton, or Banff. As well, they produced display cases and instructional manuals on art for use in schools. In 1955 Glyde resigned as chairman.

Lake Kalamalka, 1953
oil on board
cat. no. 60

Pender Island, 1964
oil on board
cat. no. 83

EXPLORATIONS • WORK IN EDMONTON

After his move to Edmonton, Glyde continued to paint landscape and went into the field whenever his busy schedule permitted. He took full advantage of the time in Banff in the summer, but the different locales of his paintings indicate summer holidays spent in other areas, for example, Lake Kalamalka and Windermere Lake in British Columbia. He also started visiting the Gulf Islands off Vancouver Island in the early 1950s. In 1954 he bought a property on Pender Island where he would later retire.

He frequently painted in oils on small panels in the field. There was an authenticity and poetic truth to these sketches. They were fresh and spontaneous with crisp colour, brighter than earlier work, and glowing with the vibrancy of oil paint. Glyde often worked directly on unsized panels. The colour was often applied in patches of paint and parts of the panel were allowed to show, giving the unity Glyde had achieved in previous work with coloured underpainting. Rhythms became less evident in favour of greater structure. Many rock, tree, and landforms were heavily outlined. *Roe's Point* 1960, is a lively oil sketch capturing the freshness of this outdoor scene.

Glyde developed a very successful method of representing water, as seen in the beautiful, luminous painting *Lake Kalamalka* 1953, in which he captures the sense of light flickering on the surface. On a yellow ground he has worked a layer of grey-green and white paint in a broad quick manner. Over this, many broad stipples of different colours, including white and a bright teal green, give an effect of moving water with shadows and reflections.

These smaller panels were worked up into larger, more structured compositions, in which his ability in handling oil paint to attain a rich and lustrious surface is evident. In *Dumbarton Rock* 1949, the surfaces are carefully built. In this painting, vibrancy is attained by the layering and breaking up of the surface, using various methods of painting: scumbling, patches of paint, cross-hatching, and modelling. Pen and ink is also used. In the later painting, *Pender Island* 1964, the luminosity is in the oil and glazing itself. This is a more formally structured work with shapes modelled in brilliant rich colours. The paint handling is much more direct. The luminous sky has a transcendant, spiritual quality, giving an intensity of mood and feeling to the whole painting.

Glyde continued painting works with epic themes. *She Sat Upon a Hill Above the City* 1949, is based on a biblical theme. A languid nude lies on an undulating ground which is cut through to reveal four cramped figures below. Two ghostly figures walk past on the left. They are insubstantial, partly transparent, and seem to float. In the distance is a typical prairie town with grain elevator and telephone poles. Energy and tension is conveyed through the contrast between the classical and serene nude and the more baroque figures below and beside her. Rhythms flow through the figures and into the background. *over*

Peace, 1949
mixed technique on masonite
cat. no. 48

The painting has a brilliant light. A bright colour effect, with a predominance of yellow and green, is attained with rich Prussian blue in the ghostly figures, making strong counterpoint to the yellow tonality. There are no deep shadows apart from the area under the ground where the sombre figures, subtly and carefully modelled, loom out of the darkness. Over the rest of the composition is an even tonality, in part due to the underpainting of a red-brown colour. This underpainting is left as an outline around the forms, providing a unity to the composition. There is no solid colour; the modelling of the volumes is cross-hatched and build up in layers. Some of the surface is rough and coarse due to a scumbled application of paint.

This painting seems to embody a philosophical reflection on the nature of life itself and is pervaded with an aura of mystery. It is an enigma eluding specific interpretation. Its mood is felt but the essence can only be grasped by an intuitive response.

Another of the large figure compositions, *Peace* 1949, demonstrates the mixed technique that Glyde had first learned from André Biéler in 1940 in Banff. The following year at the Kingston Conference, there were two chemists who discussed the mixed technique and pamphlets on it were available. In this technique the layering of tempera and glazes on an imprimatura base, provides a rich depth of colour.[1] The use of purer primary colours gives an unusually bold effect. In this work, colour has been applied in thin transparent layers with strong highlights, resulting in a richly coloured and translucent surface of great beauty.

The subject of *Peace* is dramatic and complex, with an aura of mystery about it. Contemporary Alberta is the locale, yet the scene is mythic, an allegorical rendering of the human soul's journey to salvation or damnation. In the foreground St. Michael spears the devil while in the background, a scene of worship is depicted in peaceful surroundings. The heaving graveyard at the left presages doom. The devil, part-human, part-animal, is a strong and vital image of evil. Anonymous, creature-like figures file behind him. Some enter a dark tunnel in the earth, symbol of darkness and death. Others move upwards towards the church. Stylistically, there is a juxtaposition of a calm, classical mood and a more animated discordant Baroque feeling.

The distortion seen in some of the figures in *Peace* is similar to some other mythological drawings Glyde did at this time. In some of these paintings the distortion is exaggerated to the point where the figures have an almost surreal quality.[2] The meaning of these paintings with their disturbing, non-human shapes is often not clear.

Though the subject matter of *Below Rundle, Canmore* 1950 is not epic, the effect nevertheless is consistent with that of the other epic paintings. This is one of Glyde's most accomplished paintings, a concentrated vision which conveys a moment of imaginative intensity. The composition,

Aftermath, 1952
mixed media on canvas
cat. no. 56

with its strong linear structure, is solid and classical. Quiet rhythms flow through the landscape from the curved road in the foreground to the hills and mountains in the background. There is also a certain rhythm in the repetition of groups of buildings and the repeated structural forms. A low, even light pervades the scene illuminating the buildings and providing a reflected light in the shadows. The colour is an even, warm, tonality. In this extremely simple conception, all the elements are in perfect harmony.

In *Aftermath*, painted in 1952, the theme of destruction is emphatic. Showing the streaks of jets that have just passed, it deals with Edmonton after a raid. The composition is bathed in a soft light. The rich, luminous sky carries a sense of foreboding. The landscape is shown heaving up, its dislocated buildings leaning helter skelter. Dead or distraught figures are grouped in the foreground. The drama of the idea is underscored by the composition, with the unstable angles of leaning buildings in danger of imminent collapse and turbulent movement in the figures. The curvilinear outlines of the figures adds to the aggitated feeling engendered in the forms.

Both *Bankhead* and *End of the Prairie* of the mid-fifties are different from *Aftermath*. They have a formal and coherent structure and exude a classical calm. *Bankhead* 1955 refers to a deserted mining town near Banff, where the mine was closed due to poor market conditions and an eighteen-month miners' strike. It became a ghost town. Despite the content, this is a magical, beautiful painting.

Bankhead, 1955
mixed technique on canvas
cat. no. 61

The political statement is underplayed, yet made stronger by the simplicity of the visual ideas. Ghostly figures inhabit an eerie dreamlike mountain landscape where the original buildings are implied by faint outlines of arches. A remarkable light spreads across the landscape illuminating the edges of objects and figures. The forms, particularly of the figures in this work, are severely simplified and geometric.

This abstraction is even more pronounced in *End of the Prairie* 1957, which depicts the oil refineries east of Edmonton. The human figures have been reduced to mechanical forms in a mechanical landscape. The composition is set up on a grid system and is wholly geometric. It has a deep illusionistic space. Each plane is illuminated. A beautiful rich surface is created by the layering and stippling of one colour over another, in a highly worked, dappled manner. The eerie, quivering light from the lamps pervades the scene, giving the whole a surreal effect.

The strange surreal quality of both of these works may relate back to Glyde's English experience. In the 1930s there were elements of surrealism in English painting, seen particularly in the work of Paul Nash and Edward Wadsworth. These paintings by Glyde have an imaginative, neo-romantic quality akin to Nash's. They have an eerie, surreal sense of space and yet convey the spirit of a specific place.

These two works also suggest the direction Glyde's work was to move in the late 1950s and early 1960s. He began experimenting with abstraction, manipulating form,

shape, and texture in paintings with bold primary colours. He played with different kinds of painting surfaces — thick impasto, stippling, knife-work, collage, and sand embedded in paint.

Prior to this there had been the occasional experiment in which forms approached abstraction. In *Backyard, Small Alberta Town* c.1949, leaning buildings, fences, and telephone poles are used as abstract elements. This painting has a modernist quality with something of the energy and dynamism of the Vorticists, a group of English artists working in London in the 1920s, of whom Glyde was aware. However, it is Glyde's only known painting using this particular approach.

It may be that, in the late 1950s, nearing sixty years of age, he was feeling pressure from the younger artists around him who were working in contemporary styles. His own work started to look increasingly conservative, still rooted as it was in ideas and a style developed earlier in his career.

By the 1950s in the United States, the Abstract Expressionists had removed all figurative allusions and subject matter from painting. They called attention to the two-dimensional surface of the canvas. Two streams of painting were encompassed by this movement: gestural painting, which had roots in surrealism and the automatic, intuitive or immediate process of painting; and colour-field painting which explored the expressive possibilities of colour. In Canada, ''automatic'' painting using dream images and

Backyard, Small Alberta Town, c.1949
oil on pressed board
cat. no. 46

working from the subconscious had been explored by the Automatistes in Quebec and by J.W.G. Macdonald in the 1940s, first on the west coast, then in Calgary, and finally in Toronto. Macdonald's explorations spearheaded Painters Eleven in Toronto towards an Abstract Expressionist style. Glyde must have been aware of these tendencies. Indeed, he had first-hand experience of the work of Macdonald, through his teaching at Banff.

However, Glyde's attempt to manipulate paint in a free, intuitive way failed; he was wedded to logical construction and specific drawing of forms. He was not able to let go of some kind of structure. Though some of his paintings have the appearance of surrealism, using similar formal devices and unusual juxtaposition, they are not in fact surreal in impulse or origin.

It is probable that Glyde also drew on his earlier experience of English art with the avant-garde work of Christopher Nevinson using the dynamism and repetition of forms of the Vorticists, Paul Nash's neo-romantic work, and Ben Nicholson's pure abstract style in which forms are reduced to the circle, square, and rectangle.

Glyde experimented with both deep and shallow space. In the former, the forms were abstracted and often facetted, at times appearing slightly cubist with a deep, illusionistic, surreal space. Elements of the figure as they emerge from these abstracted forms are only partly seen. In the other, geometric, flattened, humanoid figures are pressed up against the picture plane. They have a peculiar

Figures in Landscape, c.1950,
mixed technique on masonite, cat. no. 51

anthropomorphic quality. The use of primary colour is bold with sharp and often crude contrasts, quite unlike Glyde's previous work. The intensity and juxtaposition of the colour provides an abstract spatial quality.

None of these paintings become completely abstract or stripped of their figurative references. Glyde's flirtation with abstraction was with outward appearances and was decorative rather than formal. He did not apply his rigorous classical training to the reduction of forms to their essential characteristics. Though he could simplify, stylize, and modify, he could not reduce forms totally.

In general, these works are not successful, they lack the conviction and knowledge of the more naturalistic work and have an awkward and arbitrary quality. They were quite experimental and Glyde himself admits:

"I just wanted a change and did all sorts of things. It was forced in a sense.[3] I was getting in a bit of a rut... I was interested in getting texture. I wanted to superimpose one figure on another you see, and see how the patterns worked out. I learned a lot from it — in pattern-making and simplification. I'm not a colourist and I felt that I was repeating myself too often and I wanted to get stronger colour. Force an issue. But it just didn't happen. I had great fun. I'd do a lot of them. I destroyed a lot of them. I didn't exhibit any of them at all."[4]

However, some of this searching had a positive and valuable effect on his art. His work became simplified and freed of the rigid constraints of structure. He increasingly used bold patches of paint, quickly laid in, which provided

a generalized treatment and a geometric simplification which moves closer to abstraction. In *Freighter in Swanson Channel, North Pender, B.C.* c.1962, forms have been extremely simplified, the colour laid in with patches of paint. Strokes are laid vertically and horizontally in a build up of colour from yellow to blue, giving an impression of sparkling water. It is an easy transition from this to the severely abstracted painting *Rocks and Water, North Pender, B.C.* 1962. In this work, the rock forms make an abstract pattern in the foreground, the water is an open expanse of paint, and the distant land mass is laid in with horizontal and vertical bands of paint. Glyde produced few works of such severe abstraction. This is probably his most successful painting using this approach.

In the figure studies, the transition from the poetic naturalism of *Figures in Landscape* c.1950, to other styles used in later nude paintings is extremely marked. The division of the figure into distinct planes in *Reclining Figure* 1956, gives it a presence akin to the mechanical figures of the French artist Leger. The work, boldly structured with forms severely abstracted, has a monumental, classical quality.

Seated Figure 1959, an oil on a small panel, is an exceptional figure study. It is one of the few nudes treated in such a fresh and spontaneous manner and relates to landscape studies of the time. The figure and some objects behind her are outlined with a quick and sure line. Rich patches of primary colour are laid in short brush strokes.

Reclining Nude, 1960s
mixed technique on masonite
cat. no. 76

Bather, 1963
oil on canvas
cat. no. 80

Freighter in Swanson Channel,
North Pender, B.C., c.1962
oil on masonite
cat. no. 77

The simplification of forms and the spontaneous manner gives this work the feeling of the modernist painting of Cezanne.

Faceting and texturing is employed successfully in *Reclining Nude* 1960s, which still retains the structure and classicism of Glyde's best work. Thin layers of paint have been applied, mainly with the palette knife, and a rich translucent colour effect is achieved with underpaint shining through. The figure is divided into broad simple planes and the faceted background suggests an attempt to come to terms with some aspects of Cubism, particularly where one sees through and around objects. The faceting and delicate shading of each area gives an illusion of deep, though ambiguous space.

The diversity in style of all these works indicates an artist searching and trying to extend his visual vocabulary and reach.

A landscape in which the composition is so reduced it is almost abstract is *Highway No. 2 Going North* 1960, a night scene. Layers of dark colour have been built up with small cross-hatched brush strokes allowing subdued colour underneath to show through. From the flickering field of layered marks, forms seem to emerge and then disappear again in the darkness, only partly seen. There is a Whistlerian effect in the extreme simplification, the darkness, and the luminous quivering quality of the surface.

A similar cross-hatched surface is built up in *Bather* 1963, but here the form of the figure is clear and separate from the background, which is divided into simple flattened areas of colour built up with cross-hatching. This is the most successful of the semi-abstract figure studies.

Glyde's superb ability as a draughtsman is clear in the many drawings he did throughout his long career. With a quick sure line, he can capture the essence of the forms, and the varying pressure of the line describes the internal volumes.

In earlier work, apart from a few portraits, drawing generally was a means to an end, a study to be incorporated into a final composition. From the 1950s, there were more drawings for their own sake. During his year in Europe, from 1958 to 1959, he attended the Slade School and there are many life drawings from this period. Most are quick sketches showing the nuance of form as the fluid line describes the figure. He describes this line:

"I did have this tendency for a free line. I always had a feeling that there was a beginning and there was a middle and there was an end to a line. It had a pressure when you started, and you sort of begin to caress the form just a little. Then when you get into it full-blast, then you've got to end it. And it whispers away. A line that hasn't got those three parts to them, somehow to me loses its rhythm."[5]

Using this flowing line, he also did many drawings of mythical, allegorical, and biblical themes. In many of these

a witty, lively line is used. In some, there are anthropomorphic figures and settings that are often quite unnatural and imaginary. *Moses Returning From the Mountain* 1956, is a quick illustration of the idea, using an energetic line and simple intermittent washes of watercolour. It is light-hearted and whimsical, a play in line for the sheer enjoyment of drawing.

He did many large scale landscape drawings from the late 1950s. Those of the mountains are bold with a clear, well articulated structure. These confident, emphatic works convincingly translate the massive mountain form. In *Calgary Highway, Four Miles From Banff* 1967, the basic outlines are established with a sure firm line and the volumes are described by broad simple blocks of shading using the flat side of the conté drawing stick.

Many of the large line drawings incorporate a colour wash applied in limited areas, so that the work remains essentially a drawing. Quite a number of these were done during visits to England and depict the villages of Sussex, for example, the simple but lively *Poynings, Sussex* c.1968. Some are of towns and have an architectonic quality, while others convey the lyricism of nature. These are fresh and vibrant works.

Early in his career, Glyde made some block prints, first in England and then in Canada. His use of the white line technique and fine and detailed cutting is typical of the medium. The curved forms of trees, rhythmic landforms,

and robust volumetric figures give an energy to the image similar to the energy in his drawing.[6] He made a number of block prints which were used as Christmas cards.

A technique similar to the block print is scratchboard, in which the design is incised into a board with a specially prepared surface. *Headless Horseman* 1940s is an illustration in scratchboard. A lively line establishes the composition. Delicate lines pick out some of the forms. Various linear patterns, parallel, cross-hatched, and pecked out lines created shades of grey providing a delicate surface. The tones are well balanced and there is a strong compositional integration.

Amongst other things, Glyde did illustrations for various projects including *Alberta Golden Jubilee, Evergreen and Gold, Three Icelandic Sagas*, and *Rima: The Monkey's Child*. Illustrations also appeared in *The New Trail* and in calendars published by the University of Alberta.

Due to his involvement in the Studio Theatre at the University, Glyde also did some set design. In 1950, he painted panels for *Henry IV* and in 1952, he designed the set for *Rehearsal*. He also did illustrations for programs.

A Gulf Islands Wharf, Marina,
c.1981
oil on canvas
cat. no. 97

Old Buildings, East Saanich,
Vancouver Island, B.C., 1980
oil on canvas
cat. no. 96

FREE TO PAINT By 1966 the Fine Arts Department at the University of Alberta had grown tremendously and, to support it, the administration had also grown. Glyde was no longer stimulated by the university environment and was tired of the busy schedule. Also, as he admits: "I was a bad administrator. I didn't keep up with my correspondence, and I was much more interested in people and talking about things and getting things moving."[1] Furthermore, he anticipated greatly increased future enrollment, and did not want to be involved in a move to a new building. Central to his attitude though, was the desire to paint. "I had less energy of course. Plenty of ideas but much less energy. Sometimes I used to force myself to paint when I got home, and during the weekends."[2] He was also exhibiting less after 1960.

Glyde enjoyed the intimacy of things on a small scale and the feeling of being part of it all. As the institutions in Banff and Edmonton grew, he became disenchanted.

His teaching and administrative responsibilities increasingly prevented him from painting. He was also, quite simply, tired. Despite this, Glyde had been happy teaching and had felt very much at home in Edmonton. He considered that he had learned a lot from the students. "I didn't intend to teach. But I did enjoy it, I grew to really enjoy it. And incidentally, it improved me a great deal."[3] He wrote to Jackson: "When teaching full-time, little serious thought can be given to one's own painting though

students keep one young and present all kinds of new ideas."[4]

Glyde retired at the end of the school year in 1966. For his enormous contribution to art in Alberta, the University honoured him in a ceremony at the Banff School of Fine Arts, 22 July, 1966 where it conferred on him the University of Alberta National Award. Although it had been awarded to many distinguished Canadians, this was the first time it was given to an Albertan. The citation stated:

"Tonight we are proud to honour a native of England who for thirty years has been a fellow-Canadian, a great teacher, a distinguished artist, and a true gentleman, Henry George Glyde. As we present him with the Medal of the University of Alberta National Award in Art, we offer him and Mrs. Glyde our best wishes for many happy years of retirement and of creative activity in the field of the palette and the brush."[5]

Later that year the Glydes moved to their home on Pender Island, B.C. Glyde had an idea he might like to go back to England to live, and in fact, spent most of 1968 there. But ultimately, though he travelled regularly to England, he decided to remain in Canada.

On settling on Pender, Glyde initially found it difficult to get down to painting. "I'd been time-tabled for thirty years. It took ages to get it out of my system."[6] But after a few years he was able to write to Jackson:

"This is the beginning of my third year away from the work

Port Washington, Pender Island,
c.1968-69
oil on canvasboard
cat. no. 89

grind and I must say, I'm feeling much better for it. Although I've found it difficult making the complete break and my mind was for a time always wanting to hang on to the old programs, but now, the freedom is becoming precious and I hope, productive.''[7]

It was a new beginning. He cut most of his ties with the University. In the early 1970s though, he did teach a few summers at Banff, but the school had changed and he liked it less and less. There was no sense of continuity in the teaching, in following students' work as they progressed from year to year. The town had also changed. He wrote to Jackson: "The atmosphere has changed considerably since the old intimate days of the school in the town. Expansion and development gives importance in one way but much is lost in another."[8]

Glyde felt at home in British Columbia and enjoyed being at the sea again as he had been in his youth. He wrote to Jackson: "This is a lovely part of Canada. Full of islands and channels, some say it's similar to Georgian Bay."[9]

He also found new challenges and insights in the very different terrain British Columbia provided. The verdant growth and diversity of the vegetation could be overcome by simplification. It was, to his eyes:

"...a closely knit design. You get here something which is reasonably large in pattern but rich in texture. You get a bigness too when you think of the space that's beyond the trees. Lots of the stuff here is to do with man. So the high horizon that I'm using now brings all the sorts of things I want to say about where people tread. The figure has always been with me in that sense."[10]

Initially after his retirement, his work was seldom exhibited, but from the mid-1970s his work has been increasingly included in important exhibitions and seen in one-person shows. He has also had frequent and considerable popular success with exhibitions at commerical galleries in Alberta, British Columbia, and Ontario.

Glyde has worked energetically for the last twenty years producing a very large body of work. While he has not recently been tempted to return to his earlier epic-mythic themes, he continues to work with a broad range of subject matter. There are pure landscapes of the mountains, prairies and coastal regions; figures set in landscape of the rural genre and nudes. He still sketches a great deal but also uses his early sketchbooks for ideas for paintings. He produces watercolours, oil sketches, and larger finished oil paintings, but he no longer works in the more complicated and time consuming tempera, mixed media, and casein techniques. After his experiments of the early 1960s with abstract styles and varied techniques, his work has settled down and he continues to work in the more definite style of his earlier period.

His facility as a draughtsman and in paint handling has not lessened. Though the compositions themselves are still carefully orchestrated, the paint handling, possibly benefiting from his experiments, is looser, more fluid, and quite assured.

Sidney, B.C., 1970
oil on canvasboard
cat. no. 90

His recent work carries essential characteristics previously established. His compositions have a firm, logical structure with careful attention to a harmonious sense of balance and proportion. The work has become increasingly stylized, he relies more on memory and sketches than direct observation.

His watercolours, where light washes of paint are applied over pencil, are quickly rendered and light in tone. He has also produced some luscious small oil panels which are simple and fresh. His large oil paintings of the mountains are more formalized and show the impressive structure of the mountains — planar and geometric. Among the coastal scenes are paintings which show his great ability in depicting movement and light on water with quick, extremely fluid brushwork.

Later figure compositions of casual everyday scenes at the coast and on the prairies, though still composed, are more carefree and lack the rigid formal structure of earlier works. An earlier painting, however, *Port Washington* 1953, has some of the elements of the later work and seems to presage these paintings. Set at the old government wharf on Pender Island, the painting shows knots of figures casually gathered on the jetty. The sea lies in the distance. In this work, in impasto, colour and tone are united in a well balanced composition. Dark, heavy outlines define the generalized figures which are not rendered with the full volumes used in other works. They are much more two-dimensional.

This treatment of figures is seen again in his compositions of the 1970s, for example, *Sidney, B.C.* 1970, in which the figures are rather stick-like, extremely generalized with features only summarily indicated. The colour is strong and bright with rich primaries. The surface is painted more directly with fluid and blocked-in brushstrokes.

Somewhat different from these works are compositions in which the figures are bold and statuesque. In these there is a strong, simple, linear structure. A definite outline still defines the figures and other details, resulting in a rather tight composition.

Sunday Morning, North Pender 1976 is typical of these linear, bold paintings. The forms of the heavily outlined figures are cylindrical volumes with distinct planes. The forms are not modelled, the transition from solid colour to shadow is abrupt, making the figures appear mechanical. Colour areas are blocked-in, unlike the heavily worked and richly layered surface of earlier pieces.

Two Figures 1970s shows a similar linear structure which, in conjunction with the geometric background, greatly flattens the space and almost reduces the composition to a pattern.

Glyde has recently moved to Victoria though he often returns to Pender Island. He maintains studios in both locations.

Henry Glyde, c.1975

ACHIEVEMENTS In his thirty years of teaching in Alberta, Glyde made an enormous contribution. When he arrived in 1935, there were few teachers and professional artists, and the fledgling programs for art in Calgary and Banff had only recently been established, in 1927 and 1933 respectively. His students in his first years at the Institute invariably had no prior training in art. From the beginning, he showed a willingness to get involved not only at the post-secondary but especially at the grass-roots level in full recognition of the need for an overall, broad base in art. His teaching in the community classes brought many students into the art institutions, first in Banff and Calgary, and later in Edmonton. Though he had high personal standards, he did not put art on a pedestal. His democratic approach made art available to the people. His activities were on a broad and varied scale, and through them he helped establish and maintain a place for art in Alberta.

For his students at the Institute and the University, he not only provided a thorough grounding in the techniques and methods of painting and drawing, he encouraged them to see and think. Though he was demanding and set high academic standards, he was generous and open-minded, and made himself accessible to his students. Through his own enthusiasm and dedication and his enjoyment of teaching, he imbued in his students a love of art and a realization of its importance and relevance in contemporary life.

Many of Glyde's students went on to develop important careers in art. Of his earlier students in Calgary, Stanford Perrott and Stanford Blodgett became important teachers and in time, headed the Institute in Calgary. Wilfred (Roloff) Beny became a renowned artist on the national scene, while Margaret Shelton continued to produce art of conviction in this area. Of his Edmonton students, Alison Forbes became a teacher at the University, first in Education and later in Fine Arts where he headed the Art History Department. Marcel Asquin became supervisor of art programs for the Calgary School Board. Robert Wark became curator of the Huntington Library, Art Collections and Botanical Gardens in San Marino, California. Most of these students built on their initial studies by taking degrees and courses elsewhere, but they had their start in the fledgling programs under Glyde.

Glyde did not spawn artists who worked in his particular style, though there were artists like Blodgett who had a continuing interest in the figure. Nor did any of these artists continue to use the elaborate mural techniques he taught them, though many have maintained a predilection for working in watercolour. It seems Glyde's primary and overall influence was one of conveying a sense of conviction of the importance of art in enriching and enhancing life. Given the figurative and narrative emphasis in art in the 1980s, it is interesting to speculate how much greater Glyde's influence might have been at a later time.

In his work he was assisted by many others, but he remained a key player. He was particularly good at getting groups together and getting things started. He was highly respected by his peers and also by those in positions of authority.

"From the standpoint of his personality, his interest in the work, his likeability as an individual and his ability to inspire students, I have nothing but the highest recommendation."[1]

He got and kept the support of those directing art institutions and programs, who were setting policy and getting the government involved and committed. He got strong backing particularly from Dr. Carpenter in Calgary, Donald Cameron in the extension program and Banff, and Dr. Robert Newton in Edmonton.

He was nominated and appointed to serve on most of the major art organizations and committees in the province. Through his teaching, his involvement in exhibitions, and other activities he has played a major role in the development of art in the province. In 1982 he was awarded an honorary Doctorate of Law by the University of Alberta in recognition of his dedication and contribution to art in this region.

Glyde's art was rooted in ideas developed in England in the 1920s. Conservative as it was by international standards, this training nevertheless was the basis for his future developments. In Canada, his painstaking methods and techniques coalesced with his ideas and resulted in powerful original statements on man's predicament. His art was analytical. His synthesis was not intuitive, it was carefully orchestrated using specific types of compositions for particular effects. Nothing was left to chance, everything was worked out in small sketches, compositions were built up, and elements added to provide balanced, harmonious compositions.

In his work Glyde laid stress upon linear composition and gave a firm, plastic rendering of substantial form. His rigorously planned constructions have a strong coherence of design. His special methods of painting often result in a shimmering colour which vibrates with air and light. Initially based closely on ideas prevalent in English art, his work became increasingly original.

Through his early training, he placed emphasis on the figure which, in this environment, was unusual and not particularly acceptable. In Alberta what little public support existed for art was primarily for landscape painting, straight-forward and uncomplicated. This general lack of interest was discouraging to Glyde, "Figure painting is difficult. I thought the response was very poor.[2] I remember quite well people not wanting figure stuff. They thought my figures looked pretty funny."[3] This public interest in landscape steered Glyde increasingly to do pure landscape or landscape in which figures are not predominant.

Glyde retained a lifelong link with the land, established in his youth in Hastings and sustained through extensive outdoor work in Alberta and British Columbia. He put down roots and became a product of the local soil. His landscapes are the most direct presentation of his regional awareness. He captured the nature of his new environment with vivid intensity. He stripped the landscapes down to essential qualities, moods, and rhythms, deliberately excluding accidental elements. The landscape was seen through a marvelously clear light, giving a vibrancy to translucent colour. He conveyed a sense of man's link with the land, of being part of the landscape. Most of his landscapes are representations of an external reality but, at their best, they rise above natural description, expressing insight and feeling.

The figurative work, particularly of the 1940s and 1950s, is rich in imaginative power. The idea and content merge. His best works are those in which his imaginative insights are not processed into conventional paintings. They have weight and monumentality and an aura of mystery.

At the time his work was becoming established in Canada in the 1930s, there was a trend towards figurative art. All this changed after World War Two when international cross-currents pointing towards abstraction swept across the country. His own important artistic achievements were subsequently undervalued and his own sense of purpose was somewhat redirected. After the 1960s, the monumental, mythic, figurative works of genuine force and vivid power which had formed his distinctive and most original contributions were discontinued. His recent work is less complex, more direct, and accessible. He has, nevertheless, maintained his strong technical ability in works of coherent structure, making a lyrical interpretation of this region.

The hidden meaning of Glyde's major work which may be revealed by our intuitive response underlines his fundamental belief: "Art is a silent affair."[4]

NOTES

ENGLAND · THE EARLY YEARS

1. H.G. Glyde, "Community Art in Alberta," *Canadian Art*, 5(1): 30 (Autumn 1947).
2. Henry Glyde to author, tape 1 (May 1986): 1.
3. Glyde to author, 1:7.
4. Prospectus, Royal College of Art, London, 1926-27.
5. Tristram later published books on murals: *English Medieval Wall Painting*, 1944; *English Wall Painting of the Fourteenth Century*, 1955.
6. Glyde to author, 1:23.
7. Glyde to author, 1:27.
8. Some of the progressive alternative societies such as the New English Art Club established in late 19th century, had lost their verve; in fact, many members of this club had become academicians, or at least exhibited with the Academy.
9. Dennis Farr, *English Art 1870-1940* (Oxford: Oxford University Press, 1984), 233.
10. Frank Rutter, *Art in My Time* (London: Rich and Cowan, 1933), 1982.
11. Farr, *English Art 1870-1940*, 335.
12. The British interest in murals waned after the cancellation of Brangwyn's commission for the Royal Gallery of the House of Lords in 1930.
13. Artists commissioned by the Bank of England included: George Clausen, Walter Monnington, William Rothenstein, and Colin Gill; Curator of Bank of England, letter to author, 16 July 1986.
14. Gill also worked on three lunette-shaped murals depicting the receiving, moving, and weighing of bullion but Glyde did not assist on these.
15. Glyde to author, tape 2 (May 1986): 8.
16. Glyde to author, 2:10.
17. Glyde to author, 1:17.
18. Glyde to author, 2:26.
19. Glyde to author, 2:27.

CANADA · ADVENTURE AND EXPERIENCE

1. Glyde to author, tape 3 (May 1986): 11.
2. Stanford Blodgett to author, taped interview, 17 June 1986.
3. Provincial Institute of Technology and Art Yearbook, 1939-40: 47.
4. Stanford Perrott to author, taped interview, 18 June 1986.
5. Glyde to author, tape 4 (May 1986): 8.
6. Perrott to author.
7. Blodgett to author.
8. "Canadian Art Believed Still in Pioneer Stage," *Calgary Albertan*, 23 January 1954.
9. "Would Like to See Distinctive Art Develop in West." Lecture to the University Women's Club, *Calgary Herald*, 12 January 1943.
10. "Coste House: Calgary's Cultural Capitol," *Calgary Herald*, 21 September 1957.
11. The Calgary Art Association had an active program. Between October 1944 and May 1945, it held fifteen different exhibitions.
12. Glyde to author, 3: 13,14.
13. Perrott to author.
14. Glyde exhibited with the A.S.A. in 1936, 1945, 1949, and 1953.
15. Perrott to author.
16. Grace Turner to author, taped interview, 26 June 1986.
17. Canadian Art Galleries held a David Milne exhibition which was too radical for Calgary. It sold only one painting and even this was later traded for one by local artist, Roland Gissing.
18. Archie Key, "Coste House Exhibition Most Stimulating," *Calgary Herald*, 7 March 1946.
19. Glyde to author, 3: 30.
20. Glyde, "Community Art in Alberta," *Canadian Art* 5(1): 32 (Autumn 1947).
21. Glyde, "An Appreciation," Laura Evans Reid Memorial Exhibition, October 1952.
22. Alison Forbes to author, taped interview, September 1985.

CONSOLIDATION · EARLY WORK IN CALGARY

1. Glyde to author, 3: 20.
2. Glyde to author, 3: 16.
3. Glyde to author, tape 8 (July 1986): 1.
4. Glyde to author, 4: 23.
5. F.M. Norbury, "Displaying work: Calgary Artist," *Edmonton Journal*, 1 June 1944.
6. Glyde to author, tape 7 (July 1986): 14.
7. Glyde to author, 8: 5-6.
8. Glyde to author, 8: 9.

THE YUKON TRIP

1. Glyde to author, 7: 14.
2. Harry McCurry to G.M. Brown, 30 September 1943, H.G. Glyde file, National Gallery Archives, Ottawa (hereafter cited as NGA).
3. Donald Cameron to McCurry, 6 October 1943, Glyde file, NGA.
4. Glyde to McCurry, 20 November 1943, Glyde file, NGA.
5. A.Y. Jackson, *A Painter's Country* (Toronto: Clarke, Irwin, 1956), 143.
6. Ibid., 142.
7. Glyde to author, 4: 40.
8. Glyde to author, 4: 43.
9. D. Geneva Lent, "Artist Finds Human Interest Along the Alaska Highway," *Calgary Albertan*, 8 May 1944.
10. Glyde to author, 4: 36.
11. Glyde to McCurry, 20 November 1943, Glyde file, NGA.
12. Grace Turner to author, 26 June 1986.
13. Jackson, *A Painter's Country*, 1944.

RELOCATION · EDMONTON AND THE UNIVERSITY

1. Glyde to author, 8: 2.
2. Glyde to author, 8: 4.
3. Glyde to author, 4: 15.
4. Note by President Dr. R. Newton, 22 April 1944, on Donald Cameron letter to Glyde, 20 April 1944, University of Alberta Archives, (hereafter cited as UAA) 74-23: 4-11.
5. Glyde to author, 4: 13-15.
6. Cameron memorandum to Newton, 9 November 1944, UAA, 74-23: 4-11.
7. The Committee had four members: Chairman and Directors of Art, Drama, and Music. Glyde was Honorary Director of Art. Newton letter to Glyde, 12 April 1945, UAA, 74-23: 4-11.
8. Minutes of meeting of the Committee of Fine Arts, 5 May 1945, UAA, 73-46-1.
9. Memorandum, Newton to Chairman, Committee of Fine Arts, Professor Keeping, 9 July 1945, UAA, 73-46-1.

10. Memorandum, Newton to Keeping, 31 August 1945, UAA, 73-46-1.
11. Newton to Glyde, 25 April 1946, UAA.
12. Glyde to author, 4: 18. Glyde was initially Associate Professor of Art, then in 1951 became full Professor and in 1955, Chairman of Fine Arts, which included Art, Drama, and Music.
13. The prospectus for Fine Arts lists two courses of Art History and Appreciation: Art 51, dealing with primitive art to the Renaissance, and Art 52, from Renaissance to modern times. No practical courses were listed. It is probable that Glyde taught his drawing course as part of the education program. In 1946 the University had established its first four-year B.A. program and a core of students from the Education Department following on with four years specializing in art, took one or two courses per year. Helen Stadelbauer, a lecturer in Art in the Education Department, was joined by Alison Forbes in 1949.
14. Glyde to author, 6: 13.
15. Glyde to author, 6: 1.
16. Ibid.
17. Newton letter to Dean John Macdonald, Donald Cameron, and James Fowler, 22 May 1950, UAA, 68-1-981. A committee was established to study this. Members of the Institute in Calgary were concerned and resentful as they felt it a duplication of their efforts. However, after the matriculation requirement was established, they were in agreement.
18. Colleen Millard to author, taped interview, 30 April 1986.
19. Marcel Asquin to author, taped interview, 5 July 1985.
20. Ibid.
21. Forbes to author.
22. Ibid.
23. Ibid.
24. Robert Willis to author, taped interview, 20 July 1986. Extensive studies have been done on this mural. It is not certain exactly what materials and recipes were used. At the time it was said that it was to be painted in casein and damar varnish to give a feeling of a fresco painting. Edith Park, "The Rutherford Library," *The New Trail*, 9 (1): 35 (Spring 1951). Glyde notes on a Collinson letter to him that damar varnish was not used, 31 May 1981, Ring House files, UAA.
25. The mural, *When All the World was Burned*, has been relocated in the Rutherford Library.
26. Minutes of meeting, Committee of Fine Arts, 5 May 1945, UAA, 73-46-1.
27. The Council, established in 1946, was a permanent organization which was to take an interest in "any projects which may serve the cultural development of Canada." Secretary Lewis letter to Newton, 21 February 1946, UAA, 73-46-22. The Canadian Arts Council was made up of member societies which were national in character and included the Federation of Canadian Artists.
28. In May 1956, Glyde indicated that the Federation would have to withdraw from the Canadian Arts Council as it needed to reorganize. Glyde letter to Parkin, President of Canadian Arts Council, 7 May 1956, UAA, 73-46-23-1.
29. The Provincial Arts Board was established under the Cultural Development Act. This provincial body had four member boards for art, music, drama, and the library.

EXPLORATIONS · WORK IN EDMONTON

1. In the mixed technique process, a gesso surface is prepared upon which the basic design is drawn in brush and ink, roughly describing the forms with a certain amount of cross-hatching or shading. Then an imprimatura, often a light red, is rubbed into the panel providing a half-tone background for the painting. A white tempera is applied to model forms and finally, coloured oil glazes are wiped or brushed onto the surface, providing colour over the virtually monochromatic base. See Glyde tape with author, 8: 20 for a full description.
2. Examples of this distortion are *Chinook* and *Ghosts at Police Point*, not in the exhibition.
3. Glyde to author, tape 9 (July 1986): 16, 18.
4. Glyde to author, 5: 3-5. Due to the experimental and unresolved nature of these works, none are included in the exhibition.
5. Glyde to author, 7: 4.
6. A linocut *Prairie Serenade* was "tipped in" to *Maritime Art*, April 1943.

FREE TO PAINT

1. Glyde to author, 6: 7.
2. Glyde to author, 6: 9.
3. Glyde to author, 6: 7.
4. Glyde to Jackson, 16 October 1967. Jackson Papers, courtesy of Dr. Naomi Jackson Groves.
5. Citation for Henry Glyde, Banff School of Fine Arts, 22 July 1966.
6. Glyde to author, 6: 14.
7. Glyde to Jackson, 6 December 1968. Jackson Papers.
8. Glyde to Jackson, 16 October 1967. Jackson Papers. Glyde also taught some art classes in the Okanagan in central British Columbia.
9. Glyde to Jackson, 16 October 1967. Jackson Papers.
10. Glyde to author, 6: 13.

ACHIEVEMENTS

1. Cameron letter to Dean Macdonald, 1 September 1949, UAA, 78-17.
2. Glyde to author, 5: 7.
3. Glyde to author, 7: 8.
4. Glyde to author, tape 5, unpaginated.

BIBLIOGRAPHY

Bazin, Germain. *Italian Painting in the XIVth & XVth Centuries*. London: W. and G. Foyle, n.d.

Bell, Keith, Richard Carline, and Andrew Causey. *Stanley Spencer RA*. London: Royal Academy of Arts, 1980.

Berenson, Bernard. *Italian Painters of the Renaissance*. London: Phaidon, 1959.

Boulet, Roger. *A.C. Leighton: A Retrospective Exhibition*. Edmonton: Edmonton Art Gallery, 1981.

Collinson, Helen. *H.G. Glyde in Canada*. Edmonton: Edmonton Art Gallery, 1974.

_____. *H.G. Glyde, R.C.A.: Alberta, 1940's and '50's*. Red Deer: Red Deer and District Museum and Archives, 1978.

"Coste House: Calgary's Cultural Capitol." *Calgary Herald*, 21 September 1957.

DeWald, Ernest T. *Italian Painting 1200-1600*. New York: Holt, Rinehart and Winston, 1961.

Egerton, Judy. *English Watercolour Painting*. Oxford: Phaidon, 1979.

Evergreen and Gold. Illustrated by H.G. Glyde. Edmonton: University of Alberta, 1948.

Exhibition of Work by Teaching Staff of the Department of Art and Design. Edmonton: Department of Design, University of Alberta, 1985.

Farr, Dennis. *English Art 1870-1940*. Oxford: Oxford University Press, 1984.

Feaver, William. "The Sublime Eccentric." *Observer*, 14 September 1980.

Glyde, H.G. "Community Art in Alberta." *Canadian Art* 5(1): 30-34 (Autumn 1947).

_____. "A Tribute to Mrs. Reid." *Highlights* 5(3): 14-15 (December 1951).

_____. "What's Your Opinion?" *Highlights* 5(4): 13 (March 1952).

Greenfield, Valerie. *Founders of the Alberta College of Art*. Calgary: Alberta College of Art Gallery, 1986.

Greenwood, Michael. "Representational Art: Realism, Naturalism and Symbolism." *Artscanada* 33(4): 1-5 (December 1976/January 1977).

_____. "Myth and Landscape: An Introduction." *Artscanada* 35(3): 1-8 (October/November 1978).

Groves, Naomi Jackson. *A.Y.'s Canada*. Toronto: Clarke, Irwin, 1968.

Guedon, Mary Scholz. *Regionalist Art*. Metuchen, N.J.: Scarecrow, 1982.

Hardy, William George (ed). *The Alberta Golden Jubilee Anthology*. Illustrated by H.G. Glyde. Toronto: McClelland and Stewart, 1955.

Hedley, R.W. "English Art and Artists: 1939-1949." *Highlights* 3(5): 4-5 (December 1949).

Ironside, Jetske. *Spaces & Places: Eight Decades of Landscape Painting in Alberta*. Edmonton: Alberta Art Foundation, 1986.

Irwin, Wes. *The A.S.A.: A Brief History of the Alberta Society of Artists*. Calgary: The Society, 1974.

Jackson, A.Y. *A Painter's Country*. Toronto: Clarke, Irwin, 1958.

_____. "Sketching On the Alaska Highway." *Canadian Art* 1(3): 89-92 (February/March 1944).

Leighton, David and Peggy Leighton. *Artists, Builders and Dreamers, 50 Years at the Banff School*. Toronto: McClelland and Stewart, 1982.

Little, Harry Lee. *Rima: The Monkey's Child*. Illustrated by H.G. Glyde. Edmonton: University of Alberta Press, 1983.

Mandel, Eli. "The Inward, Northward Journey of Lawren Harris." *Artscanada* 35(3): 17-24 (October/November 1978).

Oakeshott, Walter. *The Sequence of English Medieval Art*. London: Faber and Faber, 1949.

Ohler, Peter. *H.G. Glyde, R.C.A.: Works from 1936-1985*. Calgary: Masters Gallery, 1986.

Pidruchney, Anna. "Travels from Edmonton to Teach Watercolour Class." *Vegreville Observer*, 28 March 1984.

Provincial Institute of Technology and Art. *Prospectus*. Calgary: The Institute, 1930-1948.

_____. *Yearbook*. Calgary: The Institute, 1930-1940.

Reid, Dennis. *Alberta Rhythm: Later Work of A.Y. Jackson*. Toronto: Art Gallery of Ontario, 1982.

Roseneder, Jan. *The A.S.A. Index 1948-1980*. Calgary: University of Calgary, 1982.

Rothenstein, John. *An Introduction to English Painting*. New York: W.W. Norton, 1965.

_____. *Modern English Painters: Lewis to Moore*. Vol. II. London: Macdonald and Jane's, 1976.

Rutter, Frank. *Art in My Time*. London: Rich and Cowan, 1933.

Spalding, Frances. "Sacred and Profane: The Vision of Stanley Spencer." *The Connoisseur* 205(805): 168-175 (November 1980).

Stainton, Lindsay. *British Landscape Watercolours 1600-1860*. Cambridge: Cambridge University Press, 1985.

Stone, R. *The Century of Change: British Painting Since 1900*. Oxford: Phaidon, 1977.

Three Icelandic Sagas. Illustrated by H.G. Glyde. Princeton: Princeton University Press for the American Scandinavian Foundation, New York, 1950.

University of Alberta. *Calendar*. Edmonton: The University, 1946-1966.

Wilkin, Karen. *Painting in Alberta: An Historical Survey*. Edmonton: Edmonton Art Gallery, 1980.

Wilmerding, John. *American Art*. New York: Penguin, 1976.

Woodcock, George. "There are No Universal Landscapes." *Artscanada* 35(3): 37-42 (October/November 1978).

UNPUBLISHED SOURCES

Alberta Society of Art. Papers. Provincial Archives of Alberta, Edmonton.

Asquin, Marcel. Interview with Patricia Ainslie. Calgary, 5 July 1985. Tape recording, Glenbow Archives, Calgary.

Bieler, Andre. Papers. Queen's University, Kingston.

Blodgett, Stanford. Interview with Patricia Ainslie. Calgary, 19 June 1986. Tape recording, Glenbow Archives, Calgary.

Forbes, Alison. Interview with Patricia Ainslie. Edmonton, September 1985. Tape recordings, Glenbow Archives, Calgary.

Gishler, Paul. Interview with Patricia Ainslie. Edmonton, 7 May 1986. Tape recording, Glenbow Archives, Calgary.

Glyde, H.G. Artist File. National Gallery of Canada Archives, Ottawa.

_____. Interview with Patricia Ainslie. Victoria, 20-24 May 1986. Pender Island, 17-19 July, 1986. Tape recordings, Glenbow Archives, Calgary.

_____. Interview with Helen Collinson. Edmonton, 31 July - 2 August 1971. Transcript, University of Alberta Archives, Edmonton.

Jackson, A.Y. Papers. Collection of Dr. Naomi Jackson Groves, Ottawa.

Lismer, Arthur. Papers. Montreal Museum of Fine Arts, Montreal.

MacDonald, Murray. Interview with Patricia Ainslie. Edmonton, 3 July 1986. Tape recording, Glenbow Archives, Calgary.

Millard, Colleen. Interview with Patricia Ainslie. Calgary, 30 April 1986. Tape recording, Glenbow Archives, Calgary.

Northern Alberta Artists. Part I: Personal Portraits. Edmonton: Access Alberta, 1983. Videotape.

Perrott, Stanford. Interview with Patricia Ainslie. Bragg Creek, 18 June 1986. Tape recording, Glenbow Archives, Calgary.

Turner, Grace. Interview with Patricia Ainslie. Calgary, 26 June 1986. Tape recording, Glenbow Archives, Calgary.

University of Alberta. Banff School of Fine Arts. Papers. University of Alberta Archives, Edmonton.

_____. Department of Extension. Papers. University of Alberta Archives, Edmonton.

_____. Department of Fine Arts. Papers. University of Alberta Archives, Edmonton.

_____. President's Papers. University of Alberta Archives, Edmonton.

_____. University Art Gallery. Papers. University of Alberta Archives, Edmonton.

Willis, Robert. Interview with Patricia Ainslie. Victoria, 20 July 1986. Tape recording, Glenbow Archives, Calgary.

Yates, Norman. Interview with Patricia Ainslie. Edmonton, 2 July 1986. Tape recording, Glenbow Archives, Calgary.

CHRONOLOGY

1906	June 18. Born Luton, Bedfordshire, England.
c.1909	Family moved to Hastings, Sussex, England.
to 1920	Attended Church of England elementary school in Hastings.
1920-23	Enrolled as a part-time student at the Brassey Institute of Arts and Sciences, Hastings.
1923-26	Continued at the Brassey Institute full-time. Studied primarily with Philip Cole, Harry Tickner, and Leslie Badham. In 1926 Glyde sat examinations at the Brassey Institute for entrance to the Royal College of Art, London. He won a scholarship to attend.
1926-30	Attended the Royal College of Art, London, enrolled in the School of Design. In 1928 Glyde received a Lewis Berger Scholarship for Architectural Decoration. He graduated in 1929, becoming an Associate of the Royal College of Art (A.R.C.A.). He received a scholarship in 1929 for a year of post-graduate studies in mural decoration. His teachers included William Rothenstein (principal); E.W. Tristram, Reco Capey, E. Dinkel in design and A.K. Lawrence; Walter Monnington, Randolph Schwabe, and Constable Alston in drawing and painting; and J.M. Worthington in architecture.
1929-31	Teacher (evenings) at Croydon School of Arts and Crafts.
1929-35	Teacher (evenings) at Borough Polytechnic, London.
1930	Student demonstrator at the Royal College of Art, assisting Reco Capey in the School of Design.
1930	Worked in the studios of the Imperial Institute, London, doing dioramas illustrating empire industries. They featured African scenes showing the copra and other industries.
1931	Marriage to Hilda M. Allwood of Hastings. They have three children.
1931	Elected member of National Society of Art Masters.
1931-32	Assisted Colin Gill with murals for the Bank of England, Threadneedle Street, London. Glyde worked on portraits of V.I.P.'s with architectural views of London as backgrounds.
1931-35	Teacher at High Wycombe School of Arts and Crafts.
1932	Elected member of Bucks Art Society.
1935	September. Arrived in Canada intending to stay for one year to teach at the Provincial Institute of Technology and Art in Calgary, Alberta. Decided to remain in Canada.
1935	November. Became a member of the Alberta Society of Artists (A.S.A.).
1936-46	Head of the Art Department, Provincial Institute of Technology and Art.
1936-47	Acted as president of A.S.A.
1936-66	Head of the painting division, Banff School of Fine Arts.
1938-39	Elected chairman of A.S.A.
1937-c.51	Taught in the Community Art classes through the Extension Department of the University of Alberta, under Dr. Donald Cameron, director.
1941	Attended the Kingston Conference at Queen's University, Kingston, Ontario.
1941	Associate of the Royal Canadian Academy.
1943	October-November. Trip with A.Y. Jackson to Yukon to record construction of the Alaska highway.
1946-66	Established and organized the Division of Fine Art, University of Alberta. In 1946 Glyde became Associate Professor, University of Alberta. He taught in the B.A. (three-year degree) and B. Ed. (four-year degree) programs and the extension classes on campus. In 1951 he became Professor of Fine Arts. In 1953 the first four-year Diploma Program in Art was initiated.
1947	Alberta delegate to the national conference of the Federation of Canadian Artists and the Canadian Arts Council.
1948	Design completed for a bas relief made for Students Union Building, University of Alberta, Edmonton.
1948-55	Chairman of Alberta Visual Arts Board, which circulated exhibitions and encouraged art throughout the province.
1948-58	Vice-President and Alberta representative to the Canadian Arts Council.
1949	First trip back to England, also visited Paris and southwest France.
1950	Elected to Royal Canadian Academy.
1950	Appointed Curator of the University Art Gallery and Museum, Edmonton.
1951	Mural completed for Rutherford Library, University of Alberta, Edmonton: *Alberta History*.
1952	Mural designed for Wauneita Lounge, Students Union Building, University of Alberta, Edmonton: *When All the World was Burned*.
1954-56	National President of Federation of Canadian Artists.
1956	Mural for the Public Library, Medicine Hat, depicting the history of the western prairie as a memorial to the pioneers. Commissioned by Mrs. Helen Gibson.
1957	Mural for City Hall, Edmonton, showing the history of Alberta, executed in aluminum in five panels from modelled bas relief mould.
1958	Awarded Canada Council Senior Fellowship. Travelled in Europe for one year to England, France, Belgium, and Italy. During this time Glyde attended the Slade School, London.
1960	Mural for St. Patrick's Roman Catholic Church, Medicine Hat: *Fourteen Stations of the Cross*.
1966	September 1. Retired from University of Alberta. Received National Medal for Painting, University of Alberta. Settled on Pender Island, British Columbia.
1967	Canadian $1 stamp reproduced from *Imperial Wildcat No. 3* by the Canadian Banknote Company Limited.
1967-68	Travelled to England.
1970-73	Instructor of Drawing, Banff School of Fine Arts, summer session.
1973	Travelled to England.
1977	Opening of Glyde Hall at Banff School of Fine Arts.
1981	Travelled to England.
1982	Awarded Honorary Doctorate of Law Degree, University of Alberta, Edmonton.
1985	Settled in Victoria, Vancouver Island.

EXHIBITIONS

SOLO EXHIBITIONS

1937 March. Hudson's Bay Company, Calgary
April. University of Alberta, Edmonton
1944 May. Calgary Art Association, Coste House
June. Edmonton Museum of Arts
June/July. Calgary Stampede
1946 March. *An Exhibition of Paintings By H.G. Glyde, A.R.C.A.*
Canadian Art Galleries for Calgary Art
Association, Coste House
1948 December. Home and School Association, Jasper
1953 January. Edmonton Museum of Arts
February/March. *Paintings by H.G. Glyde, R.C.A., A.R.C.A.*
Canadian Art Galleries, Calgary
November. Rutherford Library Art Gallery, University of
Alberta, Edmonton
December. Medicine Hat Library
1956 December. *Paintings by H.G. Glyde.* Hudson's Bay Company
Auditorium, Edmonton
1957 December. *An Exhibition of Twenty-one Watercolours
by H.G. Glyde.* City Hall, Medicine Hat. Touring through
Western Canada Art Circuit to:
1961 February. New Westminster Public Library,
March. Prince Albert Public Library,
November. Calgary Allied Arts Centre,
1962 January. Kelowna
1963 October. *Drawings by Glyde.* Studio Theatre Foyer,
University of Alberta, Edmonton
1966 May. *Henry George Glyde.* University of Alberta Fine
Arts Gallery, Edmonton
1974 December. *H.G. Glyde in Canada.* Organized by the
Edmonton Art Gallery. Touring to:
1975 June. Mendel Art Gallery, Saskatoon,
August. Peter Whyte Gallery, Banff,
October. Alberta College of Art, Calgary,
1976 January. Burnaby Art Gallery
1975 Calgary Gallery
1976 March. Backroom Gallery, Victoria
August. Vernon Art Gallery
1977 September. Masters Gallery, Calgary
1978 March. *H.G. Glyde, R.C.A. Alberta, 1940's and '50's.*
Organized by the National Exhibition Centre,
Medicine Hat. Touring to:
August. Red Deer and District Museum and Archives
1979 November. Lefebvre Gallery, Edmonton
1980 April. *This End Up: H.G. Glyde 1936-1944.* Touring to
eleven centres in Alberta for the Alberta 75th
Anniversary Commission, Alberta Culture
1980 December. The Art Emporium, Vancouver
1981 April. *Oils, Watercolours and Drawings by H.G. Glyde.*
Lefebvre Gallery, Edmonton
December. *H.G. Glyde.* Masters Gallery, Calgary
1982 February. *H.G. Glyde, 1936-1944.* Lloydminster, for the
Alberta Games Meeting
May. Hollander York Gallery, Toronto
May. *Henry George Glyde.* Jubilee Auditorium,
Edmonton
1985 April. The Art Emporium, Vancouver
1986 April. Masters Gallery, Calgary

TWO-THREE PERSON EXHIBITIONS

1942 July. Banff School of Fine Arts
1944 November. Vancouver Art Gallery
1945 December. Canadian Art Galleries, Calgary
1949 April. Calgary Allied Arts Centre, under auspices of
Canadian Art Galleries
1983 October. *Watercolours by Three Alberta Artists.* Vic Gallery,
Edmonton

GROUP EXHIBITIONS

1928 Students International Exhibition at Prague, Czechoslovakia
1944 January. National Gallery, London. Canadian art under the
auspices of National Gallery of Canada, Ottawa
April. National Gallery of Canada, Ottawa. Exhibition of
war art
1946 November. *An Exhibition and Sale of Canadian Art,* Edmonton
Museum of Arts. Organized by the Quota Club, Edmonton,
and Canadian Art Galleries, Calgary
1953 May. *R.C.A. Exhibition of Diploma Works,* National Gallery of
Canada, Ottawa
1954 November. *R.C.A. Exhibition of Diploma Works,* Art Association
of Montreal
1957 May. *Special Exhibition of Contemporary Painting.* University of
Alberta, Community Art Class Conference
Second Biennale of Canadian Art, National Gallery of
Canada, Ottawa
1963 June. *Festival Art Exhibition: Stratford Shakesperean Festival presents
Canada on Canvas.*
September. York University, Toronto
1964 *Art Rental and Sales Collection.* Edmonton Art Gallery
1967 April. University of Alberta Faculty Exhibition, Edmonton Art
Gallery
1976 September. *Through Canadian Eyes.* Glenbow-Alberta Institute
1977 Alberta Art Foundation exhibition, touring Europe, United
States, and Canada
1980 July. *Painting in Alberta: An Historical Survey.* Edmonton Art
Gallery
September. *Alberta Art.* Shell Centre Gallery, Calgary
1981 *Metaphors For Motion.* Edmonton Art Gallery, touring
1983 September. *Winnipeg West.* Edmonton Art Gallery, touring
1986 March. *Spaces and Places.* Alberta Art Foundation, Edmonton,
touring
June. Friends of the University of Alberta Museums,
Edmonton

EXHIBITIONS WITH SOCIETIES AND ASSOCIATIONS

1931 Royal Academy, London, 1931, 1932, 1933
1933 Royal Society of British Artists, 1933
1936 Alberta Society of Artists, 1936, 1945, 1949, 1953
1940 Royal Canadian Academy of Arts, 1940-1946, (1942 touring),
1948, 1951, 1952, 1955, 1957, 1958
1942 Ontario Society of Artists, 1942, 1943
Canadian Society of Graphic Art, 1942 (touring), 1951, 1958
1947 Federation of Canadian Artists, Western Canada Art Circuit,
1947, 1948
1949 Alberta Visual Arts Board, 1949, 1950

CATALOGUE OF THE EXHIBITION

Dimensions are given in centimetres, height precedes width; where two measurements are given, image precedes support measurement. Accession numbers for items in public collections are given in brackets after collection name.
Numbers for items which are included in the Glyde inventory at Ring House Gallery, University of Alberta, Edmonton, are indicated at the end of an entry.

Inscription abbreviations used:
br bottom right   cl centre left
bl bottom left   tr top right
cr centre right   tl top left

*   Denotes work illustrated.
** Denotes work illustrated in colour.

*1.   *The Resurrection*, 1927-28
study
gouache on paper
21.6 x 29.4; 28.8 x 39.2
Inscription: br ''H G GLYDE''
Private Collection

2.   *On the Way to Calvary*, 1928
study for egg tempera panel
gouache on paper
23.1 x 31.6; 28.0 x 38.2
Inscription: br ''GLYDE''
Private Collection

*3.   *Perseus and Andromeda*, 1929
egg tempera on gesso panel
38.2 x 53.5
Inscription: br ''H G GLYDE/—32—''
Private Collection
For Glenbow showing only

*4.   *A Village Church, Sussex*, 1929
watercolour over pencil on paper
39.0 x 54.4
Inscription: br ''GLYDE''; title and date verso
Private Collection
Inventory: #167

*5.   *Abingdon, Oxfordshire*, c.1931
watercolour over conté on paper
38.5 x 54.5
Inscription: br ''GLYDE''; title and date verso
Private Collection
Inventory: #164

*6.   *Hilda*, 1931
pencil, conté, brush and Chinese ink on paper
26.7 x 17.4
Inscription: br ''Glyde''
Private Collection

*7.   *Self Portrait*, 1932
conté on paper
41.1 x 32.7
Inscription: br ''Glyde/32''
Private Collection

8.   *Hilda*, c.1934
pencil on paper
26.7 x 17.4
Inscription: br ''GLYDE''
Private Collection
For Glenbow showing only

**9.   *Country Dance*, 1935
egg tempera on gesso panel
30.4 x 43.5
Inscription: br ''H.G. GLYDE/35—''
Private Collection
For Glenbow showing only

*10.   *Skaters*, 1935-36
oil on canvas
46.4 x 61.4
Inscription: br ''GLYDE''
Private Collection
Inventory: #319

*11.   *The Three Sisters*, 1936
watercolour over pencil on paper
30.0 x 37.4 (sight)
Inscription: br ''H.G. GLYDE 36.''
Collection of Mr. and Mrs. Thomas R. Stanton, Calgary
For Glenbow showing only

*12.   *Vegreville Skyline*, 1937
watercolour on paper
30.8 x 37.9 (sight)
Inscription: br ''GLYDE''; title and date verso
Collection of Wilbert (Bill) M. Hopper, D.C., Calgary
Inventory: #192

*13.   *Lunch, Vegreville*, 1938
watercolour over pencil on paper
39.8 x 48.8
Inscription: br ''GLYDE''; date verso
Private Collection
Inventory: #272

**14.   *Outskirts of Lethbridge, Alberta*, June 1938
watercolour over pencil on paper
36.0 x 26.0
Inscription: br ''Glyde''; title and date verso
Collection of Glenbow Museum
Purchased with Alberta 75th Anniversary Funds, 1980
(80.35.1)
Inventory: #471

*15. *The River Bottom*, 1938

watercolour over conté on paper
30.6 x 36.3 (sight)

Inscription: bl "GLYDE'38"

Collection of Glenbow Museum
Purchased with funds from the Glenbow Museum
Acquisitions Society, 1986 (986.85.3)

16. *Skiers, Mount Norquay*, 1938

watercolour over pencil on paper
37.0 x 50.9 (sight)

Inscription: br "GLYDE"

Private Collection
For Glenbow showing only

17. *Banff, Main Street*, 1940

watercolour on paper
38.0 x 50.7

Inscription: br "GLYDE"

Collection of the Alberta Art Foundation, Edmonton
(984.76.2)

*18. *South of Lethbridge*, 1940

watercolour on paper
31.4 x 40.3

Collection of the Alberta Art Foundation, Edmonton
(984.76.3)

Study for
*19. *The Exodus*, 1940

pencil, conté, and wash on paper
27.5 x 35.5; 27.5 x 38.1

Inscription: verso, br "Idea for Exodus —
/Flood just west of Calgary/around 1940—"

Permanent Collection, University Collections,
University of Alberta, Edmonton (974.23.14a)
Inventory: #321

*20. *The Music Group*, 1940s

oil on canvas
46.2 x 61.9

Inscription: bl "GLYDE/'40[?]"

Permanent Collection, University Collections,
University of Alberta, Edmonton (965.42)
Inventory: #459

21. *Hilda*, 1941

oil on canvas
62.2 x 56.5

Inscription: br "GLYDE/41"

Private Collection
Inventory: #310

22. *Passers By*, 1941

oil on canvas
60.4 x 77.4

Inscription: bl "GLYDE 42[?]"; title verso

Private Collection
Inventory: #118

*23. *Moving In*, 1941-42

oil on canvas
62.0 x 76.8

Inscription: br "GLYDE"

Private Collection
Inventory: #136

*24. *Sketching Group*, c.1942

watercolour and gouache on paper
26.2 x 37.2; 28.7 x 40.0

Collection of Glenbow Museum
Purchased with the Walter Phillips Collection, 1961
(61.21.449)
Inventory: #472

**25. *Manoeuvres* (Currie Barracks Road), 1943

oil on canvas
61.6 x 67.3

Inscription: bl "GLYDE 43."

Note: Glyde: "I used 24th Street as the location, a block
       south of 17th Avenue Southwest."

Private Collection

*26. *Kluane*, 1943

conté on paper
28.2 x 38.1

Inscription: br "Kluane."; signature and date verso

Permanent Collection, University Collections,
University of Alberta, Edmonton (974.23.25)
Inventory: #428

27. *Hyland River Crossing*, 1943

pencil and conté on paper
28.3 x 28.1

Inscription: cr "Bridge Construction — /Hyland River
Crossing."; title and date verso

Permanent Collection, University Collections,
University of Alberta, Edmonton (974.23.20)
Inventory: #323

28. *Alaska Highway*, 1943
Study for *Bridge Building*

pencil and conté on paper
27.9 x 37.8

Inscription: bl "70 miles/from/Coal River,";
signature, date, and title verso

Permanent Collection, University Collections,
University of Alberta, Edmonton (974.23.27)
Inventory: #430

*29. *Bridge Building*, c.1943

oil on wood panel
25.4 x 35.3

Collection of the Canadian War Museum, Canadian
Museum of Civilization, National Museums of Canada,
Ottawa

30. *Construction, Whitehorse*, 1943

oil on panel
24.5 x 34.5 (sight)

Inscription: bl "Whitehorse"; br "Glyde'43/GLYDE"

Note: Companion piece by A.Y. Jackson in National
  Gallery of Canada Collection.

Collection of Dr. and Mrs. Donald A. Grace, Calgary

31. *Camp 108, Northwest of Whitehorse*, 1943

oil on panel
24.3 x 34.6 (sight)

Inscription: bl "GLYDE"

Note: Reproduced in A.Y. Jackson "Sketching on the
  Alaska Highway." *Canadian Art*, 1 (3): 91
  (February/March 1944).

Collection of Dr. and Mrs. Donald A. Grace, Calgary

32. *Whitehorse, American Camp below the Airport*, October 1943
Study for *Alaska Highway, Northern B.C.* (cat. no. 36)

pencil, conté, and watercolour on paper
28.2 x 38.2

Inscription: bl "4.30 p.m. WHITEHORSE";
verso tl "Pencil Drawing on location/with wash";
tr "WHITEHORSE/AMERICAN CAMP/below the
airport — 1943/Oct."
Private Collection

33. a,b. *Lethbridge*, 1943

watercolour, over conté on paper
14.8 x 19.0 (image)

Inscription: br "GLYDE"

Note: a and b have the same medium, size, and inscription
Private Collection

34. a,b. *Lethbridge, West End*, 1944

a. watercolour over conté on paper
   16.0 x 19.5 (image)
b. conte
   16.0 x 27.2 (image)
Private Collection

35. *Stream, Alaska Highway, Northern B.C.*, 1944

oil on canvas
46.0 x 56.0

Inscription: bl "GLYDE/44"

Permanent Collection, University Collection,
University of Alberta, Edmonton (950.66)
Inventory: #445

36. *Alaska Highway, Northern B.C.*, 1944

oil on masonite
61.2 x 78.4

Inscription: br "GLYDE 44"; title verso

Note: Study for this is inscribed "Whitehorse American
  Camp below the airport"

Private Collection
Inventory: #119

*37. *A Main Camp, Alaska Highway*, 1944

watercolour over pencil on paper
43.4 x 52.5 (sight)

Inscription: br "GLYDE 44"; title and description verso

Collection of the Calgary Board of Education

*38. *Prairie Woman*, c.1944

oil on canvas
61.5 x 46.5

Inscription: br "GLYDE"

Collection of the Calgary Board of Education

39. *Rosebud*, 1944
Study for *Sunday, Rosebud, Alberta*

watercolour over conté on paper
27.4 x 35.8

Inscription: br "GLYDE"; colour notes around image
Private Collection

*40. *Sunday, Rosebud, Alberta*, 1945

watercolour over pencil on paper
37.1 x 47.4

Inscription: bl "GLYDE 45"

Private Collection
Inventory: #59

41. *The Flood*, 1946

egg tempera on paper
36.8 x 46.2

Inscription: br "GLYDE 46"; bl "Egg Tempera on Paper
— Sketch for 'The Flood' "
Private Collection

42. *Rosebud, Alberta*, 1947

oil on canvasboard
60.7 x 76.8

Inscription: bl "GLYDE 47"

Permanent Collection, University Collections,
University of Alberta, Edmonton (950.64)

43. *Dry River Bed, Canmore*, 1948

oil on wood panel
33.4 x 40.7

Inscription: bl "GLYDE"; title and date verso
Private Collection
Inventory: #10

**44. *Dumbarton Rock*, 1949

mixed technique, pen and ink on canvasboard
45.5 x 60.7

Inscription: title verso
Private Collection
Inventory: #1

45. *Near Luton, Bedfordshire*, 1949
oil on wood panel
33.6 x 41.7
Inscription: title verso
Private Collection
Inventory: #22

*46. *Backyard, Small Alberta Town*, c.1949
oil on pressed board
32.8 x 40.7
Inscription: br "GLYDE"
Private Collection

*47. *Kluane Lake on Alaska Highway*, 1949
oil on canvas
56.1 x 76.5
Inscription: br "GLYDE/49"
Collection of Glenbow Museum
Purchased 1956 (56.37)
Inventory: #480

*48. *Peace*, 1949
mixed technique on masonite
60.5 x 74.6
Inscription: br "GLYDE 49"
Permanent Collection, University Collections,
University of Alberta, Edmonton (950.67)
Inventory: #327

**49. *She Sat Upon a Hill Above the City*, 1949
mixed technique on cardboard
60.6 x 76.2
Inscription: bl "GLYDE/49"; title verso
Collection of Glenbow Museum
Gift of Helen Collinson, 1981 (81.50.2)
Inventory: #669

Study for
50. *Below Rundle, Canmore*, 1949
(cat. no. 54)
pencil on paper
27.4 x 37.7
Inscription: br "GLYDE"; date verso
Private Collection

*51. *Figures in Landscape*, c.1950
mixed technique on masonite
32.1 x 65.5
Private Collection
Inventory: #29

*52. *Prairie Couple*, 1950
egg tempera and oil on wood panel
40.9 x 33.4
Inscription: br "GLYDE 50"
Permanent Collection, University Collections,
University of Alberta, Edmonton (950.91)
Inventory: #328

53. *Miner's Cottage, Canmore*, 1950
oil on canvasboard
60.7 x 76.8
Inscription: title verso
Collection of The Edmonton Art Gallery
Inventory: #672

**54. *Below Rundle, Canmore*, 1951
oil on canvas
76.8 x 87.5
Inscription: br "GLYDE 51"
Private Collection
Inventory: #102

55. *Design*, 1951
pen and ink and watercolour on paper
39.7 x 43.9
Inscription: bl "GLYDE — 51"
Private Collection
Inventory: #289

*56. *Aftermath*, 1952
mixed media on canvas
81.3 x 101.8
Inscription: bl "GLYDE '52"; title verso
Private Collection
Inventory: #92

57. *Imperial Wildcat No. 3*, 1952
oil on board
33.0 x 40.8
Inscription: bl "GLYDE 52"
Note: Study for *Imperial Wildcat No. 3*, National Gallery of
Canada Collection; used as a stamp, 1967.
Private Collection

58. *Through the Keyhole*, 1952
pen and ink over mixed technique on board
40.2 x 33.0
Inscription: br "GLYDE 52"
Private Collection
Inventory: #844

59. *Port Washington*, 1953
oil on masonite
50.6 x 61.0
Inscription: br "GLYDE 1953"
Private Collection

*60. *Lake Kalamalka*, 1953
oil on board
31.9 x 39.4 (sight)
Inscription: br "GLYDE 53"
Private Collection

*61. *Bankhead*, 1955

mixed technique on canvas
82.0 x 101.5

Inscription: br ''GLYDE 55''

Collection of Government House Foundation, Edmonton
Inventory: #91

62. *High Timber*, 1955

oil on masonite
33.1 x 40.6

Inscription: bl ''GLYDE/55''; title and date verso

Collection of Glenbow Museum
Purchased with funds from the Glenbow Museum
Acquisitions Society, 1986 (986.85.2)

63. *Seated Figure*, 1955

mixed technique on masonite
40.6 x 33.3

Inscription: bl ''GLYDE''; title and date verso

Private Collection

64. *Medicine Lake*, 1956

oil on canvas
51.3 x 61.0

Inscription: bl ''GLYDE '56''; title verso

Collection of Dr. Paul Gishler, Edmonton
Inventory: #799

65. *Moses Returning From the Mountain*, 1956

pen and ink and watercolour on paper
38.7 x 56.8

Inscription: br ''GLYDE '56''

Private Collection
Inventory: #48

66. *Reclining Figure*, 1956

oil on canvas
61.2 x 76.6

Inscription: br ''GLYDE/56''

Collection of Greg P. Grant, Vancouver
Inventory: #475

**67. *End of the Prairie*, 1957

mixed technique on masonite
61.0 x 101.5

Inscription: br ''GLYDE '57''; title verso

Permanent Collection, University Collections,
University of Alberta, Edmonton (966.5)

68. *Two Figures*, 1958

pen and ink on paper
48.2 x 31.6

Inscription: br ''Glyde 58''; title verso

Private Collection

69. *Sussex Village*, c.1959

pen and ink and watercolour on paper
48.0 x 63.5

Private Collection

*70. *Steyning, Sussex*, 1959

conté and watercolour on paper
48.3 x 63.5

Inscription: bl ''Steyning — Sussex 1959''; br ''GLYDE''

Private Collection

*71. *St. Pancras Station*, 1959

chalk and watercolour over pencil on paper
58.0 x 78.0

Inscription: br ''Glyde''; title and date verso

Private Collection
Inventory: #369

**72. *Seated Figure*, 1959

oil on panel
24.5 x 19.1 (sight)

Inscription: bl ''GLYDE/59''

Collection of Snyder Hedlin Gallery, Calgary

73. *Trees, North Pender, B.C.*, 1960

soft conté and watercolour on paper
38.8 x 56.0

Inscription: br ''GLYDE''

Private Collection

74. *Roe's Point*, 1960

oil on wood panel
19.9 x 25.3

Inscription: bl ''GLYDE/1960''; title and date verso

Collection of Glenbow Museum
Purchased with funds from the Glenbow Museum
Acquisitions Society, 1986 (986.85.1)

**75. *Highway No. 2 Going North*, 1960

oil on canvas
69.4 x 84.5

Inscription: bl ''GLYDE''

Collection of Glenbow Museum
Gift of Helen Collinson, 1981 (81.50.1)
Inventory: #88

*76. *Reclining Nude*, 1960s

mixed technique on masonite
46.0 x 60.8

Inscription: bl ''GLYDE''; title verso

Private Collection
Inventory: #842

*77. *Freighter in Swanson Channel, North Pender, B.C.*, c.1962

oil on masonite
33.3 x 40.6

Inscription: br ''GLYDE''

Private Collection

78. *Rocks and Water, North Pender, B.C.*, 1962

oil on masonite
32.9 x 40.6

Inscription: br ''GLYDE 62''; title verso

Private Collection

79. *Near Bow Lake, Jasper Highway*, c.1962
conté and pen and ink on paper
27.4 x 36.9 (sight)
Inscription: br ''GLYDE''
Collection of Diana Chown, Edmonton

*80. *Bather*, 1963
oil on canvas
76.3 x 91.5
Inscription: bl ''GLYDE 63''
Private Collection
Inventory: #90

81. *Cambelltown*, 1964
oil on canvasboard
40.5 x 50.7
Inscription: bl ''GLYDE/'64''
Private Collection
Inventory: #2

82. *#4 West of Edmonton*, 1964
oil on canvasboard
40.6 x 50.8
Inscription: br ''GLYDE/64''
Collection of the Alberta Art Foundation, Edmonton
(973.6.1)

*83. *Pender Island*, 1964
oil on board
31.5 x 39.3 (sight)
Inscription: br ''GLYDE/64''
Collection of Texaco Canada Resources, Calgary
Inventory: #818

84. *West of Edmonton*, 1965
oil on canvasboard
40.6 x 50.5
Inscription: bl ''GLYDE 65''; title and date verso
Private Collection

*85. *Calgary Highway Four Miles from Banff*,
1 July 1967
conté on paper
44.0 x 58.6
Inscription: br ''GLYDE/Calgary Highway 4 miles from
Banff/July 1, 67''
Private Collection

86. *Waiting Room*, 1967
oil on canvasboard
40.7 x 51.0
Inscription: br ''GLYDE''
Private Collection

87. *Poynings, Sussex*, c.1968
watercolour and pen and ink on paper
38.0 x 46.5 (sight)
Inscription: br ''GLYDE''
Collection of Glenbow Museum
Purchased with Alberta 75th Anniversary Funds, 1982
(82.20.1)

88. *Port Washington Hamlet, B.C.*, c.1968
oil on canvasboard
40.5 x 51.0
Inscription: bl ''GLYDE''; date and title verso
Private Collection

*89. *Port Washington, Pender Island*, c.1968-69
oil on canvasboard
39.1 x 49.3 (sight)
Inscription: br ''GLYDE''
Collection of Mrs. Grace Turner, Calgary

*90. *Sidney, B.C.*, 1970
oil on canvasboard
40.5 x 50.5
Inscription: bl ''GLYDE/70''; title verso
Private Collection
Inventory: #314

91. *Piddinghoe, Sussex*, 1970
oil on canvasboard
50.9 x 60.8
Inscription: br ''GLYDE''; title verso
Private Collection

92. *Two Figures*, 1970s
oil on masonite
45.5 x 60.8
Inscription: bl ''GLYDE''
Collection of Atelier Gallery Limited, Vancouver, B.C.

93. *Elevators, Vegreville*, 1974
oil on canvas
46.0 x 61.5
Inscription: bl ''GLYDE''; title verso
Note: Based on a sketch made in 1937
Private Collection
Inventory: #650

94. *Near Coldstream, B.C.*, 1974
oil on canvasboard
41.0 x 50.8
Inscription: bl ''GLYDE''; title and date verso
Collection of Dr. Paul Gishler, Edmonton
Inventory: #809

95. *Sunday Morning, North Pender*, 1976
oil on canvas
76.3 x 61.0
Inscription: br ''GLYDE''
Collection of Greg P. Grant, Vancouver
Inventory: #1500

*96. *Old Buildings, East Saanich, Vancouver Island, B.C.*, 1980
oil on canvas
40.6 x 50.9
Inscription: bl ''GLYDE''
Private Collection

*97. *A Gulf Islands Wharf, Marina*, c.1981
oil on canvas
76.3 x 101.7
Inscription: bl ''GLYDE''; title verso
Collection of Mr. and Mrs. D.R. Taylor, Victoria

STUDIES, ILLUSTRATIONS, AND SKETCHBOOKS

*98. *Headless Horseman*, 1940s
ink on scratchboard
35.2 x 25.5
Alberta College of Art Permanent Collection, Calgary
(75.01.95)

Illustration for
99. *Three Icelandic Sagas*, c.1950
gouache on paper
49.2 x 37.9
Permanent Collection, University Collections,
University of Alberta, Edmonton (974.23.1)
Inventory: #380

Preliminary study for mural,
100. *Alberta History*, c.1950
pencil on paper
56.2 x 38.1
Note: Study of Father Lacombe
Permanent Collection, University Collections,
University of Alberta, Edmonton (974.23.13)
Inventory: #412

Preliminary study for mural,
*101. *Alberta History*, c.1950
pencil on paper
36.6 x 25.2
Inscription: cl ''Figure beside Indian.''
Permanent Collection, University Collections,
University of Alberta, Edmonton (974.23.5)
Inventory: #416

Preliminary study for mural,
102. *When All the World was Burned*, c.1952
watercolour and gouache on paper
37.6 x 26.8; 37.6 x 29.2
Inscription: br ''GLYDE''
Permanent Collection, University Collections,
University of Alberta, Edmonton (974.23.37)
Inventory: #440

Study for *The Exodus*, 1940
pencil, conté, and wash
on paper
cat. no. 19

Headless Horseman, 1940s
ink on scratchboard
cat. no. 98

Preliminary study for mural,
*103. *When All the World was Burned*, c.1952

gouache and pen and ink on paper
17.0 x 44.5; 45.6 x 62.5

Permanent Collection, University Collections,
University of Alberta, Edmonton (974.23.38)
Inventory: #441

Preliminary study for mural,
104. *When All the World was Burned*, c.1952

conté, brush and ink, and wash on paper
32.1 x 46.8

Note: Study for elk

Permanent Collection, University Collections,
University of Alberta, Edmonton (974.23.36)
Inventory: #439

Stage set for
105. *Rehearsal*, 1952

pencil on paper
27.9 x 38.0

Private Collection
Inventory: #332

Sketchbook — Alberta, British Columbia, 1950-51
106. *North End of Kalamalka*, 29 August 1951

watercolour over conté
30.2 x 22.8

Private Collection

Sketchbook — Alberta, 1951
107. *Untitled*, 31 July 1951

conté
30.2 x 22.8

Private Collection

Sketchbook — England, 1959; British Columbia and
Alberta, 1960
108. *Jasper Highway*, 1960

conté
35.7 x 25.4

Private Collection

Sketchbook — England, Winter 1973
109. *Bishopstone, Sussex*, 4 March 1973

conté and pen and ink
28.7 x 22.4

Private Collection

Sketchbook — England, 1981; British Columbia, 1982
110. *Port Washington*, August 1982

pencil
28.7 x 22.4

Private Collection

Steyning, Sussex, 1959
conté and watercolour on paper
cat. no. 70

St. Pancras Station, 1959
chalk and watercolour over
pencil on paper
cat. no. 71

LENDERS TO THE EXHIBITION

Alberta Art Foundation, Edmonton
Alberta College of Art Permanent Collection, Calgary
Atelier Gallery Limited, Vancouver
Calgary Board of Education, Calgary
Canadian War Museum,
   Canadian Museum of Civilization,
   National Museums of Canada, Ottawa
Diana Chown, Edmonton
Edmonton Art Gallery, Edmonton
Dr. Paul Gishler, Edmonton
Government House Foundation, Edmonton
Dr. and Mrs. Donald A. Grace, Calgary
Greg P. Grant, Vancouver
Wilbert (Bill) M. Hopper, D.C., Calgary
Snyder Hedlin Gallery, Calgary
Mr. and Mrs. Thomas R. Stanton, Calgary
Mr. and Mrs. D.R. Taylor, Victoria
Texaco Canada Resources, Calgary
Mrs. Grace Turner, Calgary
Permanent Collection, University Collections,
   University of Alberta, Edmonton
Private Lenders

ITINERARY OF THE EXHIBITION

9 May 1987 — 30 August 1987   Glenbow Museum, Calgary

7 November 1987 — 3 January 1988   Mackenzie Art Gallery,
Regina

4 February 1988 — 20 March 1988   Art Gallery of Greater
Victoria, Victoria

17 April 1988 — 19 June 1988   McMichael Canadian
Collection, Kleinburg

29 July 1988 — 11 September 1988   Mendel Art Gallery,
Saskatoon

12 November 1988 — 8 January 1989   Edmonton Art Gallery,
Edmonton

23 March 1989 — 7 May 1989   Art Gallery of Nova Scotia,
Halifax

This exhibition has been organized by the GLENBOW MUSEUM, CALGARY, with the assistance of the CANADA COUNCIL, the PROVINCE OF ALBERTA, and the CITY OF CALGARY.

CREDITS

Photography: Jim Shipley
Design: Mary Jameson
Typing: Kay Bridges
        Lise Dufresne
Typesetting: Luana Russell
Colour Separations: United Graphic Services Ltd.
Printing: Paperworks Press Limited